Charting Living Waters

Rhonda K. Kindig

WestBow
PRESS
A DIVISION OF THOMAS NELSON

Scripture taken from the New Revised Standard Version Bible, copyright 1989, Division of Christian Education of the National Council of the Churches of Christ in the United States of America. Used by permission. All rights reserved.

WestBow Press books may be ordered through booksellers or by contacting:

WestBow Press
A Division of Thomas Nelson
1663 Liberty Drive
Bloomington, IN 47403
www.westbowpress.com
1-(866) 928-1240

ISBN: 978-1-4497-3889-1 (sc)

Library of Congress Control Number: 2012901991

Printed in the United States of America

WestBow Press rev. date: 02/07/2012

CHARTING LIVING WATERS

Introduction

Charting Living Waters goes beyond the traditional reference books that offer maps and timelines of the Bible. The teaching materials of this manual have been developed from Bible Study groups rather than the other way around.

Learning styles do not end with childhood. We all have our preferred methods of receiving instruction, no matter our age. Youth and adults connect better with any material presented, when it is offered in varying teaching formats. The pages of Charting Living Waters offer user-friendly ideas which take differing styles into consideration so that you may easily enhance your Bible study for adults or younger learners. There are six categories:

USEFUL CHARTS For the visual learner, we all know a picture is worth a thousand words. Therefore, a chart can be the most effective means for getting information across to a visual learner. Charts also work well for analytical learners, who seek connections between things. The charts you will find herein are about connections and parallels and themes rather than geography or history. Their purpose is to provide a starting point for conversations about the Biblical narratives. It is through discussion that Scripture comes alive for learners.

UNFOLDING CHRONOLOGIES In a similar vein, the charts of this section provide information in a timeline format for Bible themes, departing from the usual listing of kings that most reference materials provide.

UNIQUE CROSSWORDS For the verbal learner, who enjoys working with words, there is a chapter devoted to unusual word puzzles designed to impart themes of the books of the Bible, through use of key verses from Scripture.

UNUSUAL CELEBRATIONS For those who need a hands-on approach, learning centers are ideal. The beauty of such centers is that they offer individually-paced learning, as well as the possibility to use the hands through interactive, manipulative activities. In addition, learning centers function beautifully in fostering cooperative learning. These might be best used in a multigenerational setting.

UNIFYING CONCEPT For both teacher and student, a "big picture" is helpful, so this short essay explains the entire "scope and sequence" of the Bible in three understandable categories.

UNIVERSAL CONSECRATION There are occasions for which you might need a devotional prayer or a closing benediction. Here are litanies which serve such a purpose.

CHARTING LIVING WATERS

Table of Contents

USEFUL CHARTS

Chronology of Each Creation Story

Genesis 1:1–2:3

God is named.

God created the **heavens** and earth.

1:2 **Spirit** of God (**Ruah**) swept over the waters.

Day One—Light

Day Two—Sky

Day Three—Earth & Vegetation

Day Four—Sun, moon, stars (to fill geography of 1st day)

Day Five—Swimming & flying creatures (to populate geography of 2nd day)

Day Six—Land creatures & humankind (to populate geography of 3rd day)

Day Seven—Rest

Genesis 2:4b–25

LORD God is named.

LORD God made the **earth** and the heavens.

2:7 **Breath** of life (**Ruah**) was breathed into his nostrils.

First—Adam from *adamah*, which is an "earthling" or creature from the earth

Second—Planted a garden (trees)

Third—Beasts of land and birds of sky

Fourth—Adam is split into man and woman, with the first use of gender-specific vocabulary

WINDOWS to the WORD

Have you noticed that particular symbols seem to recur throughout the Old and New Testaments? Images of water, bread, shepherds, and light are perfect examples of this. Some might call these icons. How would you define icon? Author Madeleine L'Engle* believed that an icon is a window to God. Lots of everyday things became icons for her, as they reflected the wonder of God. Theologian Robert Farrar Capon** has written that icons are sacraments of the very real presence of the Word of God; he even calls them God's fingerprints. Such metaphors are used in the Old and New Testaments as devices for illuminating the mystery of God. Consider the following examples and discuss how they are appropriate icons.

LIGHT

Gen. 1:3	Let there be **light**
Ex. 13:2	Pillar of fire by night to give **light**
Ps. 27:1	The LORD is my **light** and my salvation
Ps. 119:130	The unfolding of your words gives **light**
Isa. 60:3	Nations shall come to your **light**
John 1;5	The **light** shines in the darkness
John 9:5	I am the **light** of the world
Rev. 22:5	For the Lord God will be their **light**

WATER

Gen. 1:6	And God said, "Let there be a dome in the midst of the **waters**
Gen. 2:10	A river flows out of Eden to **water** the garden
Ex. 17:6	Strike the rock, and **water** will come out of it
Ps. 65;9	You visit the earth and **water** it
Ps. 107:35	He turns a desert into pools of **water**
Isa. 33:16	Their food will be supplied and their **water** assured
Ezek. 47:1-12	**Water** was flowing from...the temple
John 1:26	I baptize with **water**
John 2:9	The steward tasted the **water** that had become wine
John 4:4	The **water** that I will give will become in them springs of **water** gushing up to eternal life
John 19:34	The soldiers pierced his side with a spear, and ... blood and **water** came out
Rev. 7:17	He will guide them to springs of the **water** of life
Rev. 22:1	The angel showed me the river of the **water** of life
Rev. 22:17	Let anyone who wishes take the **water** of life as a gift

*Madeleine L'Engle, <u>Penguins and Golden Calves</u>, Shaw Books, 2003
**Robert Farrar Capon, <u>Fingerprints of God</u>, Eerdmans, 2000

BREAD

Gen. 3:19	By the sweat of your face you shall eat **bread**
Ex. 16:31,35	narrative about manna
Ex. 25:30	You shall place the **bread** of the Presence on the table before me always
Ps. 132:15	I will satisfy its poor with **bread**
Isa. 55:10	Giving seed to the sower and **bread** to the eater
John 6:1-13	Feeding the multitude
John 6:35	I am the **bread** of life
John 21:13	Jesus came and took the **bread** and gave it to them

(Bethlehem means "house of bread")

SHEPHERD--SHEEP--LAMB

Gen. 48:15	God who has been my **shepherd** all my life
Gen. 49:24	By the name of the **shepherd**, the rock of Israel
Ps. 23:1	The LORD is my **shepherd**
Isa. 40:11	He will feed his flock like a **shepherd**
John 10:11-16	I am the good **shepherd**
Ps. 100:3	We are his people, and the **sheep** of his pasture
Isa. 53:6	All we like **sheep** have gone astray
John 10:2-7	He calls his own **sheep** by name
John 21:16-17	Feed my **sheep**
Gen. 22:8	God himself will provide the **lamb** for a burnt offering
Ex. 12:5-21	Your **lamb** shall be without blemish
Isa. 11:6	The wolf shall live with the **lamb**
John 1:29,36	Here is the **Lamb** of God
Rev. 5:13	To the one seated on the throne and to the **Lamb**
Rev. 19:7-9	The marriage of the **Lamb** has come
Rev. 21:22-23	Its temple is the Lord God Almighty and the **Lamb**
Rev. 22:3	The throne of God and of the **Lamb** will be in it

GATE

Gen. 24:60	May your offspring gain possession of its **gates**
Ps. 9:13	You are the one who lifts me up from the **gates** of death
Ps. 24:7,9	Lift up your heads, O **gates**
Ps. 100:4	Enter his **gates** with thanksgiving
Ps. 122:2	Our feet are standing within your **gates**, O Jerusalem
Isa. 45:1	The **gates** shall not be closed
Isa. 54:12	Your **gates** of jewels
Isa. 60:11	Your **gates** shall always be open
John 10:7-9	I am the **gate**
Rev. 21:12-25	The twelve **gates** are twelve pearls; Its **gates** will never be shut

TREE

Gen. 1:29	I have given you...every **tree**...you shall have them for food
Gen. 2:9-3:22	The LORD God made to grow every **tree**
Gen. 3:24	He placed the cherubim...to guard the way to the **tree** of life
Deut. 21:23	For anyone hung on a **tree** is under God's curse
Ps. 96:12	Then shall all the **trees** of the forest sing for joy before the LORD
Ps. 104:16	The **trees** of the LORD are watered abundantly
Eze. 47:7-12	There will grow all kinds of **trees** for food, their leaves will not wither
Acts 5:30	The God of our ancestors raised up Jesus, who you have killed by hanging him on a **tree**
Acts 10:39	They put him to death by hanging him on a **tree**
Rev. 2:7	To everyone who conquers, I will give permission to eat from the **tree** of life
Rev. 22:2	On either side of the river is the **tree** of life
Rev. 22:14	They will have the right to the **tree** of life

SABBATH

Gen. 2:3	So God blessed the seventh day and hallowed it
Ex. 16:23	Tomorrow is a day of solemn rest, a holy **sabbath** to the LORD
Ex. 20:8	Remember the **sabbath** day, and keep it holy
Ex. 31:14	You shall keep the **sabbath**, because it is holy for you
Ex. 31:16-17	Keep the **sabbath**, observing the **sabbath** throughout their generations as a perpetual covenant. It is a sign forever between me and the people
Lev. 25:2	When you enter the land that I am giving you, the land shall observe a **sabbath** for the LORD
Deut. 5:15	the LORD your God commanded you to keep the **sabbath** day
Isa. 58:13	If you refrain from trampling the **sabbath**, from pursuing your own interests
Mt. 12:2	Look, your disciples are doing what is not lawful to do on the **sabbath**
Mt. 12:8	For the Son of Man is lord of the **sabbath**
Mk. 2:27-28	The **sabbath** was made for humankind, and not humankind for the **sabbath**; so the Son of Man is lord even of the **sabbath**
Lk. 6:9	Is it lawful to do good or to do harm on the **sabbath**
Lk. 23:54	It was the day of Preparation, and the **sabbath** was beginning
John 5:16	The Jews started persecuting Jesus, because he was doing such things on the **sabbath**

Other icons to explore: **WEDDING/MARRIAGE, STONE/CORNERSTONE, CITY/ZION,** and that uber-icon: **WORD.**

No One Is Left Behind

Numbers are used symbolically throughout Scripture; therefore, it is good to have this understanding of their significance from the opening pages.

> # 3

Three (3) represents divinity:
+ Trinity (Triune God = Father, Son, and Holy Spirit)
+ Past, present, and future tenses in the name of YHWH (Ex. 3:13-15)
+Three facets of Shema (Deut. 6:5): "You shall love the LORD your God with all your *heart*, and with all your *soul*, and with all your *might*."
+ Three gifts of the Magi (Matthew 2:11)
+ Three annual festivals requiring pilgrimages to Jerusalem for all males
+ "On the third day", used 36 times in the Old Testament and 17 times in the New, signifies God is about to do something new, i.e. Gen. 22:4; Gen. 42:18; Ex. 19:11; 2 Sam. 1:2; Hos. 6:2; John 2:1; or Acts 9:9

> # 4

Four (4) represents earthly or created things:
+ Four seasons
+ Four cardinal directions, four corners of the earth, four winds
+ Four phases of the moon each month
+ Four elements, according to the ancients: earth, water, air, fire
+ Four "living' creatures in the books of Ezekiel and Revelation
+ Four "horsemen" in the books of Zechariah and Revelation

> # 7

Seven (7) represents completion or perfection. It is obtained by adding the divine number, 3, to the earthly number, 4:
+Seven days for God to complete creation
+Sabbatical rest every 7th year for the land (Lev. 25:3-4)

Continues

+Jubilee year proclaimed after 7 (weeks) times 7 (years) (Lev. 25:8-12)
+ Seven times Joshua marched around Jericho
+ Job was blessed with seven sons (Job 1:2; 42:13)
+ Seven loaves with fishes were multiplied by Jesus (Matt. 15:36)
+ Seven baskets of food remained after the multitude was fed (Matt. 15:37)
+ Seventy times seven is the frequency for forgiveness (Matt. 18:21-22)
+ Joseph's dreams, in the book of Genesis, involved sets of seven items
+ Passover lasts seven days
+ Roman Catholics have seven deadly sins, seven virtues, and seven sacraments
+ Then, there are all those sevens in the Book of Revelation!

10

Ten (10) represents human completeness. It is obtained by adding the divine number, 3, to the complete number, 7:
+ Ten fingers
+ Ten toes
+ Basis of the decimal system
+ Basis of the metric system
+Ten commandments
+ Ten talents in Matthew's parable
+ Ten bridesmaids in Matthew's parable
+ Ten lepers healed by Jesus

12

Twelve (12) represents organized religion. It is obtained by multiplying the divine number, 3, by the earthly number, 4:
+ Twelve tribes of Israel in the Old Testament
+ Twelve disciples of Jesus in the New Testament
+ Twelve remaining baskets of food, after Jesus fed the multitude (Luke 9:17)
+ Twelve kinds of fruit on the tree of life in the Book of Revelation (Rev. 22:2)
+ Twelve pearl gates on the holy city in Revelation 21:12
+ Other religious systems also use 12: twelve signs of the Zodiac, Greeks assigned twelve deities to Mt. Olympos, Arthurian legends assign twelve knights placement at the Round Table

Continues

40

Forty (40) stands for a dimension of human suffering. It is obtained by multiplying the earthly number, 4, times 10, the number for human completeness:
+ Flood experienced by Noah began with 40 days and nights of rain
+ Israel's sojourn in the wilderness lasted 40 years
+ Moses was atop Mt. Sinai 40 days
+ Elijah was in the wilderness 40 days
+ Jesus fasted in the wilderness 40 days
+ Joseph's physicians required 40 days to embalm Jacob upon his death
+ Jonah prophesied that Nineveh would be overturned in 40 days

70

Seventy (70) represents a full dimension of completion. It is obtained by multiplying the complete number, 10, times the perfect number, 7:
+ Number of people in the household of Jacob entering Egypt (Gen. 46:27)
+ Number of years allotted to a human lifespan (Psalm 90:10)
+ Number of elders who aided Moses with leadership (Numbers 11:24-25)
+ Organization of followers sent out by Jesus (Luke 10:1-6)
+ Seventy times seven for the extent of forgiveness (Matt. 18:21-22)

6

Six (6) represents evil, since it is one short of the perfect number, 7, thereby indicating imperfection:
+It is used in this fashion in conjunction with *other* symbolic numbers rather than on its own, i.e. see "666"

Continues

3 ½

3 ½ stands for the limited supremacy of evil, since it is half of the perfect number, 7. Sometimes you need to perform some calculations to find it!
+ Both Daniel 7:25 and 12:7 refer to "a time, two times, and half time", with "time" actually standing for the word "year". Thus, the verses are suggesting 3 ½ years.
+ The "forty-two months" mentioned in Rev. 11:2 can be understood as 3 ½ years.
+ The "one thousand two hundred sixty days" mentioned in Rev. 12:6 may also be understood as 3 ½ years.
+ Rev. 11:11 specifically mentions "three and a half days".

666

666, as a function of six (6), is symbolic of the highest evil. Just as Roman numerals represent both the alphabet as well as numbers, Hebrew letters also have numeric meaning. The substitution of numbers for letters, as in a name, is called gematria. Many scholars believe 666 is gematria for Nero, a vicious persecutor of Christians (Rev. 13:18).

144

144, as the product of 12 x 12, indicates the peak of organization:
+ In Rev. 21;17, the wall of the holy city is 144 cubits.

1,000

One thousand (1,000), as the product of 10 x 10 x 10 (or 10-cubed), is the most perfect number:
+ "With the Lord one day is like a thousand years, and thousand years are like one day" (2 Peter 3:8)

+ The dragon is bound for 1,000 years (Rev. 20:2)
+ The martyrs reigned with Christ for 1,000 years (Rev. 20:4)

Also, the shape of a cube (10 x 10 x 10) is considered to be perfection:
+ In Ezekiel's 47th chapter, the measurement of the temple is described as 1,000
        cubits square
+ In 1 Kings 6:20, the dimensions for the Holy of Holies within Solomon's Temple
        form a perfect cube
+ The holy city in Rev. 21:16 is described as a perfect cube; therefore, the holy city
        is perfection

144,000

144,000 represents the ultimate totality. It is obtained by multiplying several
        excellent numbers: 12 x 12 x 1000. (Or, imagine what that would be in
        expanded notation…remember that!) The concept of a million was not really
        developed prior to the Middle Ages, so when 144,000 is encountered in the
        Book of Revelation (Rev. 7:4 or 14:1,3), it is just the largest number possible.
        No one is left behind!

HOW GOD IS ADDRESSED IN GENESIS

Reference	English	Hebrew	Notes
1:1, 46:3	**God**	elohim	"the" God ("E" Source)
2:4, 4:26, etc.	**LORD**	YHWH	YHWH is used nearly 7,000 times in the Bible. It appears in every time period. ("J" Source) *
2:4	**LORD God**		Same usage as YHWH
14:18-20	**God Most High**	El Elyon	El = high god of Canaanite Pantheon, worshipped in pre- and early Israelite times.
15:2,8	**O Lord GOD**	adonay	Lord over all (formal address)
16:13	**El Roi**		God Who Sees—as named by Hagar
17:1, 28:3, 35:11, 43:14, 48:3	**God Almighty**	El Shaddai	Name of God used by early ancestors before they learned the name YHWH. ("P" Source) Also translates as "God, the one of the mountains", or "God of the deities" (shadday), and even "God with breasts" (fertile God)
21:33	**Everlasting God**	El Olam	Ancient divine name once associated with the sanctuary at Beer-sheba. Also, "God of eternity"
33:20	**God, the God of Israel**	El-Elohe-Israel	

It is in the third chapter of Exodus that we find the story of the name YHWH being revealed and explained to Moses. The name is a verb of being that occurs simulateously in three tenses (past, present, and future)! The consonants "YHWH", which sound like a breath of air, were too holy to be spoken aloud, so in subsequent times, translators took the Latin equivalents of the letters (J-H-V-H) and added vowels between to come up with the name "Jehovah".

OLD COVENANTS and NEW

Name	Verse	Parties	Promise	Condition	Sign
Noah/ Noahic	Gen. 6:18 Gen. 9:8-17				
Abraham/ Abrahamic	Gen. 7:1-12				
Mosaic/ Sinai	Ex. 20:1-21				Hint: Ex: 31:12-17
Davidic/ Messianic	II Samuel 7:12-16				
New	Luke 22: 17-20				

Are each of the above different covenants or facets of the same covenant? Are all covenants with God ones of grace? Are there other covenants in Scripture?

     Is Jeremiah 31:31-34 a new covenant?

     Is Gen. 21:8-21 a covenant?

     Is Revelation 21:1-7 a new covenant?

(Completed chart follows.)

Name	Verse	Parties to the Covenant
Noah/ Noahic	Genesis 6:18 Genesis 9:8-17	God Noah Noah's Descendants All Creation
Abraham/ Abrahamic	Genesis 7:1-12	God Abraham
Mosaic/ Sinai	Exodus 20:1-21	God People of Israel
Davidic/ Messianic	II Samuel 7:12-16	God House of David
New	Luke 22:17-20	Jesus "YOU"
?	Jeremiah 31:31-34	
?	Genesis 21:8-21	
?	Revelation 21:1-7	

(Left-hand side of chart)

AND NEW_____

Promise	Condition	Sign of the Covenant
Nevermore a flood to destroy the earth	Unconditional	Rainbow
Will be ancestor of nations; land of Canaan will be a perpetual blessing	"Walk in my ways and be blameless." (Genesis 17:1)	Circumcision
LORD will be their God and will dwell amidst them	Follow "Torah"	Sabbath (Ex. 31:12-17) a perpetual sign!
Steadfast love and a throne established forever	Unconditional	Messiah (the anointed one)
Forgiveness of sin	"Do this in remembrance of me"	Lord's Supper of bread & wine

(Right-hand side of chart)

These Are the Generations

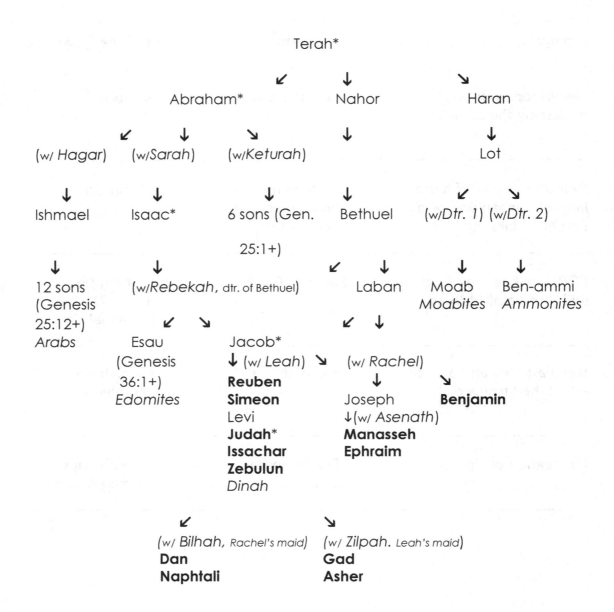

Terah*

Abraham*   Nahor   Haran

(w/ *Hagar*)   (w/*Sarah*)   (w/*Keturah*)   Lot

Ishmael   Isaac*   6 sons (Gen.   Bethuel   (w/*Dtr. 1*) (w/*Dtr. 2*)

25:1+)

12 sons   (w/*Rebekah*, dtr. of Bethuel)   Laban   Moab   Ben-ammi
(Genesis   *Moabites* *Ammonites*
25:12+)
Arabs   Esau   Jacob*
        (Genesis   (w/ *Leah*)   (w/ *Rachel*)
        36:1+)   **Reuben**
        Edomites   **Simeon**   Joseph   **Benjamin**
                 Levi   (w/ *Asenath*)
                 Judah*   **Manasseh**
                 Issachar   **Ephraim**
                 Zebulun
                 Dinah

(w/ *Bilhah*, Rachel's maid)   (w/ *Zilpah*. Leah's maid)
Dan   **Gad**
Naphtali   **Asher**

Asterisks denote the direct ancestors of Jesus.
Bold-faced names are the "Twelve Tribes" of Israel (Levites were the priests).

MATRIARCHS, not PATRIARCHS

Matriarch	Eve	Sarah	Rebekah	Rachel
Herstory (not History!)				
Tenuousness of Life; God Remembers!				
Barren Woman Tradition				
Endangered Matriarch				
Will God speak to a *woman*?				
Wimpy Patriarch? (Does what he's told!)				
Playing Favorites with the kids				
Am I my brother's keeper?				

(Completed chart follows.)

Matriarch	Eve	Sarah
*Her*story (not History!)	Mother of humankind	Mother of nation
Tenuousness of Life; God Remembers!	Gen. 3:16—"labor"	
Barren Woman Tradition		Gen. 17:17; Gen. 18:15
Endangered Matriarch		Gen. 12:10-20
Will God speak to a *woman*?	Yes Gen. 3:13, 16	Yes Gen. 18:11-15
Wimpy Patriarch? (Does what he's told!)	Yes Gen. 3:6	Yes Gen. 21:10
Playing Favorites with the Kids	Gen. 4:1-10 Cain vs. Abel	Ishmael vs. Isaac
Am I my brother's keeper?	First Murder	Rivalry & hatred to this day!

(Left-hand side of chart)

24

PATRIARCHS

Rebekah	Rachel
Mother of tribes	Mother of deliverer
Gen. 25:21-22	Gen. 30:22
Gen. 26:1-16	
Yes	
Gen. 25:23	
Yes	("tricks her father")
Gen. 27	Gen. 31:19-35
Esau vs. Jacob	Joseph vs. elder half-brothers
Deceit & trickery Alienation	Jealousy, rivalry—brother is sold into slavery. However, the last word is **FORGIVENESS!**

*After all the rivalries, hatreds, tricks, and even murder, Genesis ends on a grace note of forgiveness. Am I my brother's keeper? YES; that's the "punch-line" of the whole book.

(Right-hand side of chart)

PARALLELS between HAGAR & ISRAEL

HAGAR
Was an Egyptian slave

ISRAEL
Will be slaves in Egypt

Was degraded by Sarah

Will be degraded by Egyptians

Was told by an angel to
return to Sarai where she will
still be oppressed

God told Abraham his descendants would be
enslaved and oppressed (Gen. 15:13)

She was given the promise of
her descendants forming a
great nation

Was given the promise of multitudinous
descendants who would bless all nations

She will wander thirsty in
the desert; God will provide
water

The people will wander thirsty in the
wilderness; God will provide water

So, the destiny of Israel is not that removed from the people surrounding them!

Information for this chart was drawn from the essay, "Sarah and Hagar" by Tikva Frymer-Kenslay, in Chapter 6 of Talking about Genesis: A Resource Guide, *First Main Street Books, 1996.*

Parallels between the Perils of Ishmael & Isaac

Hagar/Ishmael (Gen. 21:14-21)	Abraham/Isaac (Gen. 22:1-18)
Begins in the morning	Begins in the morning, with Abraham rising
Needed items were placed on Hagar's back	Needed items were placed on Isaac's back
Solemn journey into the wilderness	Solemn journey into the wilderness
Abraham did not plead with God as he did for Sodom	Abraham did not plead with God as he did for Sodom
Angel calls out before the son dies	Angel calls out before the son dies
They are rescued	They are rescued
Her eyes are opened	His eyes are opened
She sees a well right there	He sees a ram right there
There is a naming: Hagar names God (Gen. 16:14)	There is a naming: Abraham named the site (Gen. 22:14)
A great nation will be made of him.	With descendants as numerous as the stars, all nations will be blessed by them.

Note: It is also interesting that in the Koran, there is also a story about Abraham binding his son for a sacrifice, but that son is Ishmael in their narrative. Another interesting tidbit is that Jewish legend is that Mt. Moriah, the place of Isaac's binding, is the same location as the Temple Mount in Jerusalem.

Information for this chart was drawn from Genesis *by David W. Colter in the Berit Olam Series (Studies in Hebrew Narrative Poetry), Liturgical Press, 2003, p. 148.*

STORYLINE of EXODUS

God's Instructions	First Response	As a Result
FIRST TRY *Exodus chap. 3-4* Moses to "Go to Pharaoh" to get people's freedom from slavery	*Exodus chap. 5* No luck— just more oppression	*Exodus chap. 7-15* So, God intervenes with plagues, the Passover, and the escape across the Red/Reed Sea
SECOND TRY *Exodus chap. 19-24* Israel is to be God's holy people	*Exodus chap. 32* No faith— golden calf incident	*Exodus chap. 34* So, God intervenes to re-establish his covenant
THIRD TRY *Exodus chap. 25-31* Israel to build a tabernacle for God's presence	*Exodus chap. 35-39* Offerings of the people and work of the artisans	*Exodus chap. 40* So, the people did just as they had been commanded!

THE PLAGUES IN EXODUS

Reference & Source	Warn Pharaoh?	Moses or Aaron?	Plague and Extent (Goshen?)	Pharaoh's Reaction	Natural Phenomenon	Mockery of Polytheism?
7:14-24 (J,P,E)						
7:25-8:15 (J,P)						
8:16-19 (P)						
8:20-32 (J)						
9:1-7 (J)						
9:8-12 (P)						
9:13-35 (J,E)						
10:1-20 (J,E)						
10:21-29 (J,E)						
12:29-36 (J,P,E)						

(Completed chart follows.)

THE PLAGUES

Reference & Source	Instructed to Warn Pharaoh?	Moses or Aaron?	Plague and Extent (Goshen included?)
7:14-24 (J,P,E)	Yes	Moses; then Aaron	Nile into blood; water into blood
7:25-8:15 (J, P)	Yes	Aaron	frogs
8:16-19 (P)	No	Aaron	gnats
8:20-32 (J)	Yes	Moses	flies (Goshen spared)
9:1-7 (J)	Yes		livestock pestilence (Israel's spared)
9:8-12 (P)	No	Moses	boils
9:13-35 (J,E)	Yes	Moses	hail (Goshen spared)
10:1-20 (J,E)	Yes	Moses	locusts
10:21-29 (J,E)	No	Moses	darkness 3 days (Goshen spared)
12:29-36 (J,P,E)	Yes	LORD	death of firstborn

(Left-hand side of chart)

IN EXODUS

Pharoah's Reaction	Natural Phenomenon?*	Mockery of Polytheism?
Pharoah did not take this to heart	Pfisteria Kills fish	Anuket of Nile Hapi of Nile
Heart hardened	Bufo toads leave river	Nu had head of frog
Heart hardened	Gnats that lead to 5th plague	
Heart hardened	Stable flies that lead to 6th plague	
Heart hardened	African horse sickness	Hathor, a cow deity
Heart hardened	Glanders	
Heart hardened	Records report large hailstorms occasionally	
Heart hardened	Records report swarms of locusts historically	
Heart hardened	Khamsin, a severe Sandstorm	Re, sun deity
Go!	Toxic mold due to grain storage issues, caused by plagues 7, 8, & 9	Pharaoh self-proclaimed

*A theory by Dr. John Malloy and Curtis Marr, described in the May 1996 issue of *Caduceus*, is also reported by Anne Raver in her April 4, 1996 *New York Times* article, "Biblical Plagues: A Novel Theory", postulating natural explanations such as these.

(Right-hand side of chart)

31

ZONES of HOLINESS

From the time of Moses onward, holy spaces have been set aside with "degrees" of holiness.

"Then the LORD said to Moses, "Go down and warn the people not to break through to the LORD to look; otherwise many of them will perish. Even the priests who approach the LORD must consecrate themselves or the LORD will break out against them." Moses said to the LORD, "The people are not permitted to come up to Mount Sinai; for you yourself warned us, saying, 'Set limits around the mountain and keep it holy.'" (Exodus 19:21-23) Also see Exodus 24:1-2.

Mount Sinai:

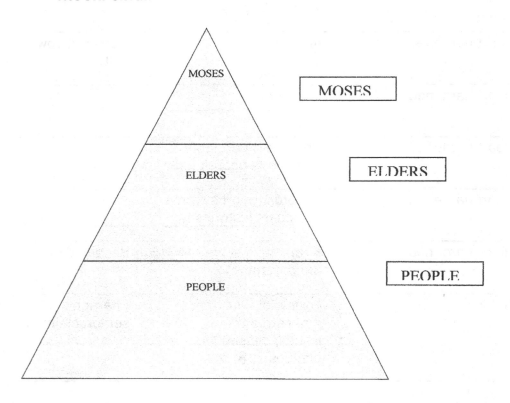

ZONES of HOLINESS

Following instructions in Exodus 35:4-40:33, the Tabernacle is constructed according to degrees of holiness. The holiest spot, the Ark of the Covenant (containing the tablets with the commandments) is innermost and restricted. Only the priests had access.

When the Temple is built under Solomon, as described in I Kings 6:17-19 and 8:6-11, a similar plan is followed. Innermost, the Holy of Holies, containing the Ark of the Covenant, was only approached once a year by the High Priest.

Ezekiel's vision of God's perfect temple, in Ezekiel's chapters 40-42, also includes zones of holiness.

Just as zones of holiness were evident at Mount Sinai, the mountain of the LORD; within the Tabernacle, the dwelling place of the LORD; and the Temple of Solomon, the House of the LORD, the entire world was conceived in degrees of holiness, with the Holy of Holies, containing the Ark of the Covenant, at the sacred center of creation. Tradition even had this as the "navel" of the world.

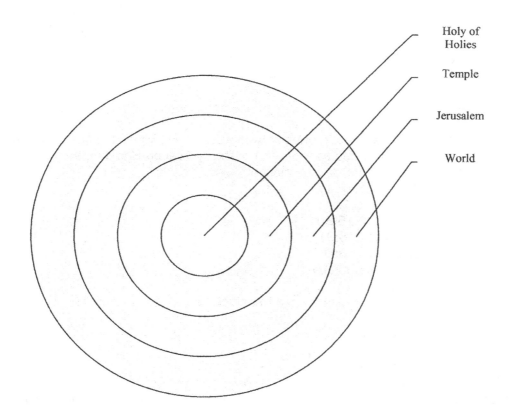

Holy of
Holies

Temple

Jerusalem

World

WE CANNOT FREE OURSELVES

The LORD raised up a deliverer.

Then Israel did what was evil in the sight of the LORD, forgetting the LORD their God.

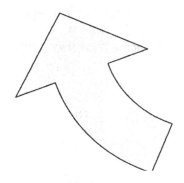

The Israelites cried out to the LORD.

The book of Judges contains the stories of twelve so-called judges, though the Hebrew word might be better translated as "deliverer"! The cyclical pattern diagrammed above is evident in the formula that introduces most of the narratives:

        Judges 2:11,16,17
        Judges 3:7,9,11
        Judges 3:12,15,30
        Judges 4:1,3; 5:31
        Judges 6:1,7; 8:28
        Judges 10:1,3,6,10
        Judges 13:1

Then the formulaic pattern changes, as a transition to the next historical books of the Bible:

        Judges 17:6
        Judges 18:1
        Judges 19:1
        Judges 21:25

"In those days there was no king in Israel; all the people did what was right in their own eyes."

A PATTERN for ISRAEL'S IDEAL KING

	I. IDENTIFICATION/ NOMINATION	II. VICTORY OVER OPPRESSION	III. PROCLAMATION/ ACCLAMATION
THE IDEAL (DIVINE MODEL)	Exodus 3:7-12 Promise of Deliverance	Exodus 14:30-31 Egypt is vanquished	Exodus 15:1-21 Song of Miriam—first instance of God called KING
THE MONARCHY (HISTORIC MODEL)	1 Sam. 9:15-17 Saul anointed by Samuel	1 Sam. 11:5-11 Saul defeats the Philistines	1 Sam. 11:12-15 Saul is proclaimed the king
	1 Sam. 16:1-13 David anointed by Samuel	1 Sam. 17:1-58 David defeats Goliath	2 Sam. 5:1-3 David is proclaimed the king
THE PROMISE (MESSIANIC MODEL)	Old Testament prophets proclaim his coming Isa. 11:1-3	Prophecy of a great battle to defeat the oppressor Isa. 13:4-6	Restoration of the glorious kingdom of David Isa. 9:6-7
THE FULFILLMENT (JESUS CHRIST)	Matt. 3:16-17	Matt. 28:5-7	Matt. 28:16-20
	Rev. 5:9-13	Rev. 21:3-4	Rev. 7:16-17

Who's Who in the Camps of Saul & David

(Important Characters in I and II Samuel)

Abigail—negotiated with David and became his wife after becoming widow to Nabal; mother of Amasa & Chileab

Abiathar—son of Ahimelech, who escaped the slaughter of the priests of Nob and joined David's outlaw band, where he served as private chaplain; David later rewarded him by appointing him chief priest

Abinadab--a prominent man from Kireath-jearim, who had custody of the Ark after its return from the Philistines, until David moved it to Jerusalem

Abishai—son of Zeruiah (David's sister) and brother of Joab; he was also a military leader

Abner—son of Ner, cousin to Saul, who was Saul's army commander; he kept a remnant of Saul's Kingdom together after Saul's death; eventually he abandoned this position and negotiated a pact with David

Absalom—son of David and Maacah; avenged the rape of his sister Tamar by his half-brother Amnon, When David took no action; led a revolt against David

Adonijah—son of David and Haggith; sought throne with support of priest Abiathar and commander Joab but was frustrated by half-brother Solomon

Ahimelech—priest of Nob who gave David holy bread and Goliath's sword; killed by Saul's command

Ahinoam—Jezreelite who married David and mothered his eldest son, Amnon

Amnon—eldest son of David & Ahinoam; coveted and raped his half-sister Tamar; murdered by Absalom

Asahel—son of Zeruiah (David's sister) and brother of Joab; he served in David's bodyguard & was murdered by Abner

Bathsheba—wife of Uriah the Hittite, coveted and seduced by David, widowed due to David's intrigue; mother to Solomon

Ishbaal (Ishbosheth/Eshbaal)—fourth son of Saul; attempted to rule after Saul's death, supported by Abner but was rejected by Judah (south); was murdered by two of his own henchmen

Joab—most prominent son of David's sister Zeruiah; commander of David's army; assassinated Abner

Jonathan—son of King Saul, bosom friend of David; died in battle against Philistines on Mt. Gilboa with his father

Mephibosheth—Jonathan's crippled son, who is treated kindly by David

Merab—elder of Saul's two daughters; promised to David (when Saul assumed David would be killed in confrontation with Philistines), but given to Adriel as wife instead

Mica—son of Mephibosheth/grandson of Jonathan/great-grandson of Saul

Michal—younger daughter of Saul, given to David as wife, later given by Saul to Palti, but returned to David; quarreled with David over his behavior before the Ark; died childless

Nathan—prophet to David

Solomon—also named Jedidiah, second son to David and Bathsheba (the LORD took the life of the first); ultimately succeeded David as king

Tamar—daughter of David and Maacah; raped by her half-brother Amnon; avenged by her full brother Absalom

Uriah—Hittite married to Bathsheba; he was an honorable warrior in David's army

Zadok—priest under David; he supported Solomon following David's death

Zeruiah—According to I Chron.2:16, she was David's sister; she was mother to Joab, Abishai, and Asahel, three of David's warriors

A KING—LIKE OTHER NATIONS

SAMUEL (Last Judge, anointer of kings)

<u>PROPHET</u>--Nathan

Tribe of Benjamin
SAUL (son of Kish)
↓   ↘
               Abner (cousin &
                 general)
↳ Jonathan
   ↳ Mephibosheth
      ↳ Mica

↳ Ishbaal/Ishvi

↳ Malchishua

↳ Merab (daughter,
   promised to David, but
   given to another)

↳ Michal (daughter,
   given to David, but
   then given to another)

PRIESTS
Ahimelech
↓
Abiathar
+
Zadok

Tribe of Judah
DAVID (son of Jesse)
↓   ↘Zeruiah (sister)
            ↳ Joab (nephew
               & general)
            ↳ Abishai (neph.
               & warrior)
            ↳ Asahel (neph.
               & body guard)

w/ Ahinoam
   ↳ Amnon

w/ Abigail
   ↳ Chileab
   ↳ Amasa

w/ Maacah
   ↳ Absalom
   ↳ Tamar (daughter, raped by
      Amnon)

w/ Haggith
   ↳ Adonijah

w/ Michal (childless)

w/ Bathsheba
   ↳ Solomon

w/ Abital
   ↳ Shephatiah

w/ Eglah
   ↳ Ithream

YHWH'S GREAT MEDIATORS

MOSES

ELIJAH

Exodus 14
    Parting the Red (Reed) Sea
	II Kings 2:8
	    Parting the Jordan River

Exodus 34:28
    Atop Mt. Sinai
    40 days and 40 nights
	I Kings 19:4-9
	    Atop Mt. Horeb (Sinai)
	    40 days and 40 nights

Exodus 16:1-30
    Provision of manna
	I Kings 17:14-16
	    Provision of jars of oil &
	    meal

Exodus 16:13
    Quails show up (as food)
	I Kings 17:4-6
	    Ravens show up (with
	    food)

Numbers 11:1-3
    God calls down fire/Moses
    intercedes
	II Kings 1:9-14
	    Elijah calls down fire

Exodus 33:17-23
    On mountain, Moses has a
    theophany—with Moses in a rock
    cleft, God passes by
	I Kings 19:11-12
	    On mountain, Elijah has a
	    theophany—first a wind,
	    then an earthquake, then a
	    fire and then God spoke in
	    the silence

Deut. 34:5-6
    No human witnessed Moses'
    death; he is buried by God
	II Kings 2:11-12
	    Elijah ascends into heaven
	    in chariots of fire and a
	    whirlwind

Comparisons between Moses and Elijah may also be found in Reading the Old Testament by Lawrence Boadt, Paulist Press, 1984.

TWICE THE SPIRIT

Two early prophets, Elijah and Elisha, are known only for the stories about them and not for any written words they left. As the successor to Elijah, Elisha had desired twice the spirit of Elijah. Judging by the number of miracles we have in the books of I and II Kings, he apparently got his wish.

ELIJAH

II Kings 2:8
Struck the water with his mantle, and it parted

I Kings 17:14-16
Jars of oil and meal never empty as provision for widow

I Kings 17:17-24
Widow's son is restored to life

II Kings 2:11-12
Elijah ascends in chariots of fire

ELISHA

II Kings 2:14
Struck the water with his mantle, and it parted

II Kings 2:19-22
Added salt to water to restore its wholesomeness

II Kings 4:1-7
Jar of oil is filled so woman can pay her debts

II Kings 4:32-37
Woman's son is restored to life

II Kings 4:38-41
Miraculous pot of stew

II Kings 4:42-44
Twenty loaves of barley feed 100

II Kings 5:1-27
Naaman is cured of leprosy

II Kings 6:1-7
Miraculous floating axe head

II Kings 6:17
Chariots of fire appear in defeat of Arameans

The Four Living Beings of Ezekiel

First mentioned in Ezekiel 1:4-10, the four living creatures will show up again in John of Patmos' book, Revelation 4:6-9. Through the centuries, fascinating layers of meaning have been assigned to these four living beings.

SOURCE	MAN	LION	OX	EAGLE
St. Irenaeus of Lyons (120-202 AD)–as symbols of Christ:	Christ's dispensation in his advent as a human being	Christ's dispensation in his royal power and leadership	Christ's dispensation of sacrificial and holy order	Christ's dispensation in the gift of Holy Spirit that hovers over us
Also Irenaeus– as symbols of the Evangelists:	Matthew, opening with Jesus' ancestry as son of men	John, whose gospel is full of confidence	Luke, which opens with the priest Zechariah giving offering (like a calf)	Mark, opens with prophetic spirit coming down from on high
Also Irenaeus– symbols of the covenants:	Adam, father of humanity	Noah, with power over animals	Moses, since ox was the sacrificial animal of the old covenant	Gospel— that raises and bears upon wings into the heavens
St. Augustine of Hippo (354-430 AD)—as symbols of the design of each Evangelist	Mark– Christ comes as a man rather than a king or priest	Matthew– Brought the kingly nature of Christ to us; Lion was symbol of Judah	Luke– Objective was to show priestly matters, like consecration	John– "Soars like an eagle above the clouds of our infirmity"
St. Jerome (347-420 AD)— as symbols of the opening of each Gospel (Jerome is best known for translating the Bible into Latin.)	Matthew opens with genealogy of Christ's human ancestors	Mark begins with voice crying out in the wilderness, like a lion	Luke offers the sacrifice by the priest Zechariah	John "Soars into the mystery of incarnation & contemplates it as profound- ly as an eagle flying toward the sun"

The illustrated and illuminated manuscripts which were being made in the Medieval Era followed Jerome's allocations, often opening each Gospel with a painting of one of the symbolic creatures.

Continues

Continued

SOURCE	MAN	LION	OX	EAGLE
Rabanus Maurus Magnentius (780-856 AD) Archbishop of Mainz, who wrote an encyclopedia	Theme of Christ's humanity: Matthew begins with genealogy for incarnation as man	Theme of Christ as king: Mark opens with John the Baptist preaching like a roaring lion	Theme of Christ as priest/sacrifice: Luke begins with temple duties of Zechariah, including sacrifice	Theme of Christ's divinity: John offers a "higher" level of theology than the three "terrestrial" gospels
Also Rabanus— as the nature of Christ	Emphasizes his human nature	Legend claims lions slept with eyes open, so Jesus, in the tomb, did not sleep	In his Passion and Crucifixion, Jesus is both sacrifice and high priest	Represents Jesus' Ascension
Also Rabanus— as the virtues needed for conversion	Christians should use their reason for salvation	Christians should be courageous on the path to salvation	Christians must be prepared to sacrifice themselves to follow Christ	Legend says eagles could look directly at the sun when flying, so Christians must look on eternity without flinching

During the Renaissance Era, the four cherubim are often found in stained glass and cathedral stonework, especially above portals.

Ezekiel, when he had the visions, had been an exile in Babylonia for six years, long enough to become familiar with the prevailing culture. Part of that culture included astrology. Although we use Latin names for the constellations in the Zodiac, of our 12 astrological signs, four of them are called "fixed" signs. These are: Aquarius (a man holding a water jug), Leo (the lion), Taurus (the bull), and Scorpio (a scorpion for us, but an alternate understanding is Aquila, the eagle). With the Earth in the center, this forms an interesting shape:

THE APOCALYPTIC TENSE
Found in Daniel

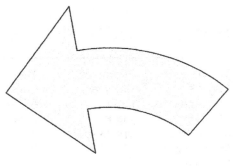

The author
takes an event
from the
PAST

To warn his
readers of
an existing
danger in the
PRESENT

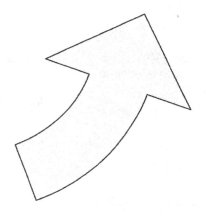

And he
predicts it
as an
event in
the FUTURE

The author of Daniel, in approximately the 2nd century BC, took an event from the past (the destruction of the Temple by the Babylonians), predicted it as a future "Coming Day of the Lord", to warn those of his generation of the evils of Antiochus Epiphanes, who had desecrated the Temple.

Some centuries later, the author, John of Patmos, in the late 1st century AD, took an event from the past (again, the destruction of the Temple by the Babylonians), predicted it as a future "Coming Day of the Lord", to warn those of his generation of the evils of Roman persecution.

Note, the "Coming Day of the Lord' denotes movement, but it is not a calendar countdown toward destruction. Rather, it is always movement BY God toward his people, which is on-going and never-ending.

Zechariah's Visions of Ever-Extended Cosmic Reign

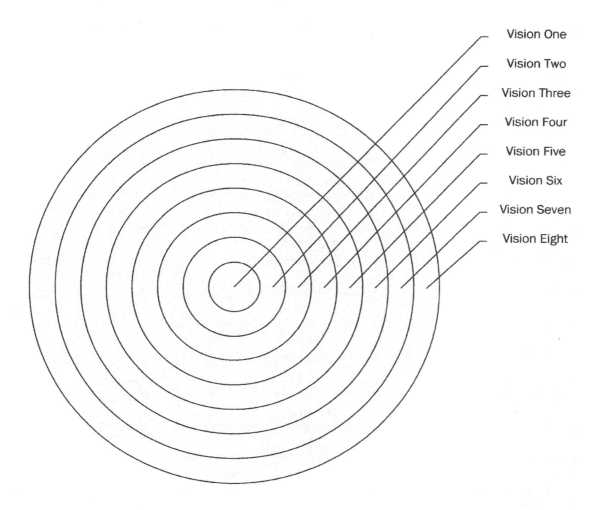

Vision One
Vision Two
Vision Three
Vision Four
Vision Five
Vision Six
Vision Seven
Vision Eight

One: Expectant Earth is patrolled by four horsemen
Two: Powerful nations were terrorizing God's people
Three: Preparation to restore New Jerusalem
Four: Heavenly court–LORD has chosen Jerusalem; the Satan is rebuked
Five: Lampstand represents God's presence
Six: Scripture (i.e. Law) emerges as the standard
Seven: Wickedness is contained and banished
Eight: Chariots patrol the Earth; the Messianic leader is crowned.

Who's Who Among Old Testament "Visionaries"

Character	Angel(s)	Visions(s)	Dream(s)
Abram		Gen. 15	
Hagar	Gen. 16,21		
Lot	Gen. 19		
King Abimelech			Gen. 20
Abraham	Gen. 22		
Jacob			Gen. 28
Pharaoh			Gen. 41
Jacob			Gen. 46
Moses*	Exodus 3		
Balaam's Donkey	Numbers 22		
Balaam	Numbers 22		
Gideon	Judges 6		
Samson's Mother	Judges 13		
David	II Samuel 24		
Solomon			I Kings 3
Elijah	I Kings 19		
"	II Kings 1		
Nathan		I Chronicles 15	
Isaiah		Isaiah 1:1 +	
Jeremiah		Jer. 1:14 +	
Ezekiel		Eze.1:4-28 +	
Daniel			Daniel 2
King Nebuchadnezzar			Daniel 2
Meshach, Shadrach, & Abednego	Daniel 3		
Daniel	Daniel 6		Daniel 7 +
"	Daniel 9		
Obadiah		Obadiah 1	
Nahum		Nahum 1	
Habakkuk		Habakkuk 2	
Zechariah			Zechariah 1-12

(Dreams were also considered "night visions".)

*Aaron and Miriam, in Numbers 12:6, are told by God that He appears in visions and dreams to prophets but face-to-face only with Moses.

Who's Who Among New Testament "Visionaries"

Character	Angel(s)	Visions(s)	Dream(s)
Joseph			Matt. 1,2
Wise Men			Matt. 2
Zechariah	Luke 1		
Mary	Luke 1		
Shepherds	Luke 2		
Jesus	Matt. 4 Mark 1 Luke 22		
Wife of Pontius Pilate			Matt. 27
Mary Magdalene, Guards	Matt. 28		
Mary Magdalene	John 20		
Apostles	Acts 5		
Ananias		Acts 9	
Philip	Acts 8		
Cornelius	Acts 10 (called a vision)		
Peter	Acts 12	Acts 10	
Paul		Acts 26	Acts 16,18
John of Patmos		Revelation (visions with angels)	

Themes in Mark's Gospel

+   Written about 68AD in Rome; actual author is unknown; possibly for a Gentile audience, since Jewish practices are explained, i.e. 7:3-4. (It is possibly the teachings of Peter.) It was the **first written** Gospel.

+   The **shortest** of our four Gospels, it begins with a proclamation of its purpose—the good news, then it jumps right into the ministry of John the Baptist in the wilderness, with no birth narratives about Jesus.

+   It is told with **unusual urgency**, leaving you breathless! The word immediately is used 42 times, compared to Luke's single use of the word.

+   Emphasizes Jesus' **deeds over his words;** teaching takes proportionately less space than other Gospels. There is a "crush" of people seeking healing.

+   Some of the **best-known stories are missing**, such as Jesus' birth, the Sermon on the Mount, the Beatitudes, the Lord's Prayer, the parables of the Good Samaritan and Prodigal Son.

+   **Motif of secrecy/mystery** is evident—the reader is aware from the beginning, but those closest to Jesus throughout remain unaware; Jesus tells people not to tell (1:43-44; 5:43; 7:36; 8:30; 9:9).

+   **Disciples** seem not only **obtuse** and unperceptive but often oppose Jesus (8:33 9:33-34;10:37-38) and **fail him** (9:17-19;14:32-41;14:50;14:66-72).

+   **Very human Jesus** is portrayed (i.e. tired in 6:31; hungry in 11:12; angry in 3:5; indignant in 10:14; limited in 6:5).

+   **Use of irony**—the disciples are continually unperceptive, yet "little people" recognize Jesus, i.e. blind men are able to see Jesus; Syro-Phoenician woman, etc.

+   **Less refined linguistically** in Greek (i.e. Mark 6:1 literally translates, "He went away from there and comes to his own country.").

+   Nevertheless, author has an **effective rhetorical style**, as represented by:

--narrative anticipations which act like glue (i.e. 3:9—have boat ready—prepare us for 4:1—beside sea)

--two-step progressions (i.e. 1:32—when it was evening, after the sun set; 1:35; 1:42; 8:17; 4:39; 8:15)

--intercalation (sandwiching stories within stories) (i.e. John's martyrdom within disciples' successes)

--triple repetitions: 3 great prophecies of passion, 3 times Jesus returns to sleeping disciples in Gethsemane, 3 accusations of Jesus before High Priest, 3 times Peter denies Jesus, and 3 times Pilate appeals to people to free Jesus.

+   **Passion dominates**: chapters 1-13 are fast-paced, but chapters 14-16 slow down to practically an hour-by-hour account. (Some have called Mark a passion narrative with an extended introduction!)

+   **Ending is abrupt**—it ends with only the empty tomb, leaving the reader curious and questioning. A later editorial longer ending will be shown in your Bibles.

+   Geographical **focus on Galilee** rather than Jerusalem. It begins and ends in Galilee.

+   **Kingdom of God**/Reign of God is Jesus' main topic throughout.

+   Mark consists of 661 verses, 80% of them appear in Matthew; 60% appear in Luke.

Themes in Matthew's Gospel

+   Written between 75-85 AD in Syria Palestine. The audience was former Jews.

+   It **preserves Mark** (all but 60 verses of it!), though it is twice the length of Mark, and it has reorganized, abbreviated, and improved the style of Mark, correcting inaccuracies. Matthew idealizes Jesus and the disciples, while disparaging the Jewish leaders.

+   Highlights the **Jewish origin** and **identity** of Jesus. There is a strong **Jewish orientation** (i.e. 10:5; 15:24; 17:24-27; 23:2-3), Semitic words are seldom explained (i.e. 5:22), as if assuming the audience already knew them.

+   Frequent **use of scripture and quotations**; shows Jesus as **fulfillment of prophecy.**

+   Tension with authorities regarding tradition and **interpretation** of law, as well as outright **hostility** to Jewish leaders (i.e. 12:34; 23:33; 9:4; 12:34; 16:4; 15:13; 21:43).

+   Illustrates examples of "higher righteousness" (i.e. Joseph, Uriah, Jesus).

+   Jesus mentions people of **little faith** (i.e. 6:30; 8:26; 14:31; 16:8; 17:20) contrast with those of **great faith** (i.e. 8:10 and 15:28).

+   **Peter** is prominent; Jesus mentions the **church** explicitly (16:17-20).

+   **Five Discourses** (five big chunks of teaching—totaling 620 verses)—Matthew likes to organize the book into patterns.

+   Jesus is **more dignified**; human emotions seem lacking.

+   Geography is not stressed, but **Galilee** is important—the Jewish area whose border Jesus scarcely crosses; after the resurrection, Galilee becomes the gateway to the world, with Jesus appearing there (not Jerusalem) as glorified and sends out disciples.

+   **Presence of God** is over-riding motif.

Information about differences among the four Gospel accounts may be found in Fortress Introduction to the Gospels by Mark Allan Powell, Fortress Press, 1998.

Themes in Luke's Gospel

+   Written between 75-85 AD in Antioch. The audience was Gentiles. It shares 220 verses in common with Matthew. The author, Luke, was not an eye-witness to Jesus; he was possibly a **physician** (based on Col. 4:14). Luke also wrote Acts. When paired with the **sequel** Acts, the two books comprise ¼ of the New Testament! Luke was a **skilled writer**; he uses 800 words uniquely in the NT. Luke was also a good **historian**, identifying both people and events.

+   The stories about Jesus in Luke anticipate the stories about the church in Acts. If both were outlined, the parallels in themes and outright actions would be staggering. And, both books begin by identifying an audience—Theophilus (God-lover).

+   **Half** of Luke's Gospel is **unique** to him—many all-time favorite stories are only found in Luke—nativity with shepherds and angels; Good Samaritan, Prodigal Son. Luke uses **unique names** for Jesus, too: Savior, King, Master.

+   Luke is the source of some of our **liturgical** elements, i.e. Nunc Dimittis; Magnificat; Benedictus; Gloria.

+   The gospel begins and ends with **worship**/in Temple.

+   Special place for the **marginalized** (downtrodden, disadvantaged, distressed)—Jesus sets people free to have the life God intends for them.

+   **Women** figure more prominently in Luke's writings, both Luke and Acts.

+   **Prayer** is a central theme (3:21; 5:16; 6:12; 9:18; 11:1) with Luke.

+   Long **travel narrative** to Jerusalem is the heart of the Gospel; **Jerusalem** is central, the Holy City, Jesus' destination. The Gospel begins and ends in the Temple in Jerusalem. Ministry is not something one goes to do, it is what occurs on the way!

+   Work of the **Holy Spirit** is emphasized. Jesus is conceived by it, anointed by it; people are filled with it and inspired by it.

+   Jesus is **eating** frequently in this Gospel, as well as talking about eating (banquet stories!)—eucharistic ties.

+   Proper use of **money** and possessions is a favorite theme.

+   **Idealizes** Jesus and the disciples. From the first chapters, Jesus is called Messiah, Savior, and Lord. And, Jesus is in control during Passion story.

+   **Salvation** is NOW (today); salvation centers on Jesus' life, as well as his death, and upon following him.

Themes in John's Gospel

+   Written about 90 AD in Ephesus as **catechism** for community of John; actual author unknown.

+   Martin Luther's favorite!

+   Follows **different chronology** of events. John begins with cleansing Temple, whereas Mark, Matthew, and Luke place this near the end of Jesus' ministry. John also has the crucifixion on a different day!

+   **90% of John is unique**, i.e. wedding at Cana, raising of Lazarus, foot-washing; along with **glaring omissions**—no nativity, no baptism of Jesus, no temptation of Jesus, no parables, no exorcisms, no institution of Eucharist

+   **Extended conversations** with people, like Nicodemis or Samarian woman at well. Conversations reflect **dualism**, light/dark; above/below; spirit/flesh; now/future.

+   **Seven great I Am the… Metaphors.**

+   **Seven signs** (not miracles, signs show the **glory** of God). Only two of these are also found in the Synoptics: Feeding the 5,000, and Calming the Stormy Sea.

+   **Seven I Am** Statements (openly identifies himself with God).

+   **Motif of misunderstanding and irony** (born again; rebuild this temple in 3 days).

+   **Journey** from Galilee to Jerusalem is background.

+   **Salvation** begins now and flows into the future (realized eschatology).

Additional information about themes in the four gospels may be found in Mark Allan Powell's Fortress Introduction to the Gospels, *Fortress Press, 1998.*

The TEMPTATION of CHRIST

Deepening Levels of Understanding

Scene One	Scene Two	Scene Three
Wilderness (Matt. 4:1-11)	Temple	Mountain overlooking world
Temptation to satisfy physical needs	Temptation to use super-natural resources	Temptation to dominate the world
Prevailing expectation of a **prophetic** messiah, one who would spread a great banquet	Prevailing expectation of a **priestly** messiah, one who would descend from the temple to rule	Prevailing expectation of a **political** messiah, one who who would rule from Jerusalem
Considers the "**heart**" (i.e. center of physical being) aspect of **Shema*** (think "lifeblood" not Valentine)	Considers the "**soul**" (i.e. center of spirit) aspect of **Shema***	Considers the "**might**" (i.e. center of strength) aspect of **Shema***

*Shema = "Hear, O Israel: The LORD is our God, the LORD alone. You shall love the LORD your God with all your heart, and with all your soul, and with all your might." (Deuteronomy 6:4-5)

Scene One	Scene Two	Scene Three
Jesus responds with Deut. 8:3 Son of God will not abuse his status for self-preservation	Jesus responds with Deut. 6:16 Son of God refrains from using his power to protect against death	Jesus responds with Deut. 6:13 Son of God refuses to exercise dominion against God's will or compromise with evil

In each case, the temptation is a preparation for the great temptation to come, the temptation to come down from the cross (Matthew 27:42).

The FIRST TEMPTATION–PARALLELS with ADAM

Scene One	Scene Two	Scene Three
First Adam failed to withstand sin in tasting the forbidden fruit	First Adam failed to withstand sin in wishing "to be like God"	First Adam failed to withstand sin in wishing to know good and evil
Jesus, as the New Adam, triumphs over the devil's temptation to eat	Jesus, as New Adam, triumphs over the devil's temptation to prove he is Son of God	Jesus, as New Adam, triumphs over devil's temptation to rule with him in any compromise

---

Continued

PARALLELS to ISRAELITES in the WILDERNESS FORTY YEARS

Longing for the fleshpots of Egypt; dissatisfaction with their food (Exodus 16:4)

Clamoring for water and putting God to the test (Exodus 17:1-7)

Idolatrous worship of the golden calf (Exodus 32)

As a reversal, Jesus will not provide himself food

As a reversal, Jesus will not use magic for proof

As a reversal, Jesus will not worship Satan

HIS OWN TIME & PLACE
JESUS OFFERS A NEW & IMPROVED RESPONSE

However, in feeding the five thousand, Jesus DOES use his power to provide food

However, instead of leaping from the temple and not dying, Jesus dies and then is resurrected

However, rather than world dominion with the devil, Jesus is glorified at the right hand of the Father ultimately

*(See **Romance of the Word** by Robert Farrar Capon, Eerdmans, 1996, for more on the idea that Jesus refused to be manipulated by the tempter, yet in his own time and place offered an improved version of each suggestion.)*

THE WORD MADE FLESH

Even though there is no story of the temptation in John's Gospel, here are fascinating possibilities:

In the Gospel of John, Jesus goes beyond the tempter's suggestion in embodying a metaphoric understanding:

In the Gospel of John, Jesus goes beyond the tempter's suggestion in embodying a metaphoric understanding

In the Gospel of John, Jesus goes beyond the tempter's suggestion in the promises he fulfills:

"I am the bread of life."
John 6:41

"Destroy this temple and in three days I will raise it up."
John 2:19

"Take courage, I have conquered the world."
John 16:33

In Order to Fulfill What Was Written

Gospel writer Matthew wishes to show how Jesus has fulfilled what had been spoken by the Lord through the prophets. Listed are specific examples of this.

Matt. 1:23	Look, the virgin shall conceive and bear a son, and they shall name him Emmanuel.
Source	Isaiah 7:14

Matt. 2:5-6	And you, Bethlehem, in the land of Judah, are by no means least among the rulers of Judah; for from you shall come a ruler who is to shepherd my people Israel.
Source	Micah 5:2

Matt. 2:15	Out of Egypt I have called my son.
Source	Hosea 11:1
Parallel	Obvious parallel to story in Exodus

Matt. 2:17-18	A voice was heard in Ramah, wailing and loud lamentation, Rachel weeping for her children; she refused to be consoled, because they are no more.
Source	Jeremiah 31:15
Parallel	Obvious parallel to story in Exodus

Matt. 2:23	He will be called a Nazorean.
Source	No corresponding Old Testament passage

Matt. 3:3	The voice of one crying out in the wilderness: Prepare the way of the Lord, make his paths straight.
Source	Isaiah 40:3
Parallel	Mark 1:2-3; Luke 3:4-6

Matt. 4:14-16	Land of Zebulun, land of Naphtali, on the road by the sea, across the Jordan, Galilee of the Gentiles— the people who sat in darkness have seen a great light, and for those who sat in the region and shadow of death light has dawned.
Source	Isaiah 9:1-2

Matt. 8:17	He took our infirmities and bore our diseases.
Source	Isaiah 53:4

Continues

Matt. 12:17-21	Here is my servant, whom I have chosen, my beloved, with whom my soul is well pleased. I will put my Spirit upon him, and he will proclaim justice to the Gentiles. He will not wrangle or cry aloud, nor will anyone hear his voice in the streets. He will not break a bruised reed or quench a smoldering wick until he brings justice to victory. And in his name the Gentiles will hope.
Source	Isaiah 42:1-4

Matt. 13:14-15	You will indeed listen, but never understand, and you will indeed look, but never perceive. For this people's heart has grown dull, and their ears are hard of hearing, and they have shut their eyes; so that they might not look with their eyes, and listen with their ears, and understand with their heart and turn— and I would heal them.
Source	Isaiah 6:9-10
Parallel	Luke 8:10

Matt. 13:35	I will open my mouth to speak in parables; I will proclaim what has been hidden from the foundation of the world.
Source	Psalm 78:2

Matt. 21:4-5	Tell the daughter of Zion, Look, your king is coming to you, humble, and mounted on a donkey, and on a colt, the foal of a donkey.
Source	Zechariah 9:9

Matt. 26:46	But all this has taken place, so that the scriptures of the prophets may be fulfilled.
Source	No specific text

Matt. 27:9-10	And they took the thirty pieces of silver, the price of the one on whom a price had been set, on whom some of the people of Israel had set a price, and they gave them for the potter's field, as the Lord commanded me.
Source:	Zechariah 11:13

Note that 3rd, 4th, and 14th events do not correspond to the other New Testament accounts of Jesus' life.

CHIASTIC STRUCTURE
For MATTHEW'S GOSPEL

A Genealogy, linking story to past (1:1-17)
  B Story of Mary; Message of Angel; Birth of Jesus (1:18-25)
    C Gifts from Magi (2:1-12)
      D Descent into Egypt (2:13-21)
        E Judea Avoided (2:22-23)
          F Jesus' Baptism—"This is my Son, the Beloved" (3:1-17);
            Wrestling with Satan (4:1-11); Sermon (5:1 – 8:1)
            G Crossing Galilee (8:24-28)
              H John's Ministry (11:2-19)
                I Rejection of Jesus (11:19)
                  J Thanks to God for Revealing Truth to Infants (Followers) (11:25-30)
                    K Attack by Pharisees (12:14)
                      L God's Chosen Servant (12:14-21)—"This is my beloved..."
                    K' Attack by Pharisees (12:22-45)
                  J' Revealing Truth to Disciples (13:1-52)
                I' Rejection by Hometown (13:57-58)
              H' John's Death (14:1-12)
            G' Crossing Galilee (14:22)
          F' Jesus' Transfiguration—"This is my Son, the Beloved" (17:1-8);
            Rebuking Demon (17:14-23); Sermon (chapter 18)
        E' Judean Ministry (19:1 – 20:34)
      D' Ascent into Jerusalem (21:1 – 22:56)
    C' Gift of Tomb (27:57-66)
  B' Story of Mary; Message of Angel; Death of Jesus (28:1-15)
A' Commission, linking story to future (28:16-20)

Found throughout the Bible, chiasmus is a symmetrical literary structure with concentric parallels of events, topics, or even phrases, in which the central concept or turning point is found in the center. In this instance, the central idea is who Jesus is—the beloved son of God, in whom God is well pleased, and the fulfillment of Old Testament prophecy.

Information about the chiastic structure within Matthew's Gospel may be found in articles by James B. Jordan, "Biblical Horizons Newsletter", No. 94, April 1997, and No. 95, May 1997. These articles may be read on www.biblicalhorizons.com

CHIASTIC STRUCTURE
For MARK'S GOSPEL

A   Galilee—place of ministry (1:9)

  B   Identified by God—Son of God (1:11)

    C   Rending of Heavens (1:10)—direct access to God

      D   Temptation of Christ (1:12-13)—suffering alone in wilderness

        E   Gathering, Calling, Appointing Twelve Disciples (3:13-19)

          F   Feeding the Five Thousand—"blessed...broke...gave" (6:39-44)

            G   Confronting the Purity Codes (7:1-12)

              H   Peter's Confession—Jesus Is the Messiah (8:29)

                I   Healing a Blind Man (8:22-26)

                  J   Passion Foretold (8:31-32)

                    K   **TRANSFIGURATION**—God's Great Mediators

                  J'   Passion Foretold (9:30-32; 10:32-34)

                I'   Healing a Blind Man (10:46-52)

              H'   Triumphal Entry into Jerusalem—Acclamation of Messiah (11:1-11)

            G'   Confronting Temple Use with "Cleansing" (11:15-19)

          F'   Last Supper—"blessing...broke...gave" (14:17-25)

        E'   Betrayal, Denial, Desertion by Twelve Disciples (14:43-45, 50, 66-72)

      D'   Crucifixion of Christ (14:16-47)—suffering alone on cross

    C'   Rending of Temple Curtain (15:38)—direct access to God

  B'   Identified by Roman Soldier—Son of God (15:39)

A'   Galilee—place of ministry (16:17)

To be found throughout Scripture, chiasmus is a symmetrical literary structure with concentric parallels of events, topics, or even phrases, in which the central concept or turning point is found in the center. In this Gospel, the turning point is the Transfiguration, where the timeless intersects with the timebound.

For additional information about chiastic structure in Mark:
> <u>Decoding Mark</u> by John Dart, Trinity Press International, 2003.
> <u>Preaching Mark</u> by Robert Stephen Reid, Chalice Press, 1999.

For a "primer" of chiastic structure:
> <u>Literary Structures of the Old Testament</u> by David Dorsey, Baker Academic, 2004.

Luke's Liturgies

A canticle is a song from the Bible apart from the Psalms:

Canticles of Deliverance	Canticles in Luke	Canticles from Revelation
Sing with All the Women of God!		Never-ending Songs!
Following an accepted understanding that women made up the choir, these are representations of a pattern called "Songs of Deliverance"—canticles with similar themes of God's bringing down the mighty and lifting up the lowly.	Luke 1:67-79 **Benedictus**	Revelation 4:8 **Trisagion (Sanctus)**
	Luke 2:14 **Gloria**	Revelation 5:12-13 **Dignus Est Agnus**
	Luke 2:28-32 **Nunc Dimittis**	Revelation 7:12 **Seven-fold Praise**
	Luke 19:38-40 **Benedictus, Qui Venit**	Revelation 11:17 **Song of Thanksgiving**
Exodus 15:21 **Miriam's Song** (Only a later editor's addition attributed this to brother Moses.) ⇨⇨⇨⇨⇨⇨⇨⇨⇨⇨⇨⇨⇨⇨⇨⇨⇨⇨⇨⇨⇨⇨		Revelation 15:3-4 **Song of Moses!** **Magna et Mirabilia** (So, the beginning is the ending, all the mighty acts of God culminate in the Lamb.)
Judges 5:1-31 **Deborah's Song** (the very oldest portion of the Old Testament)		
I Samuel 2:1-10 **Hannah's Magnificat**		
Luke 1:46-50 **Mary's Magnificat** ⇨⇨⇨⇨⇨⇨	Luke 1:46-50 **Magnificat**	

ORGANIZING the PARABLES of JESUS

Parables of the Kingdom *These parables suggest where to find the kingdom of God.*
(Note that 4/5 of these parables are found in Matthew's 13th chapter.)
+The Sower and the Seed (Mt. 13:1-9; Mk. 4:1-9; Lk. 8:4-8)
+The Lamp (Mt. 5:15; Mk. 4:21-25; Lk. 8:16-18)
+The Growing Seed (Mk. 4:26-29)
+The Weed (Mt. 13:24-30)
+The Mustard Seed (Mt. 13:31-32; Mk. 4:30-32; Lk. 13:18-19)
+The Yeast (Mt. 13:33; Lk. 13:20-21)
+The Treasure Hidden in a Field (Mt. 13:44)
+The Pearl of Great Price (Mt. 13:45-46)
+The Net (Mt. 13:47-50)
+The Householder (Mt. 13:51-52)

Parables of Grace *These parables refer to how the kingdom of God operates!*
(Note that most of these parables are unique to Luke's Gospel.)
+Coin in Fish's Mouth (*an enacted parable*) (Mt. 17:24-27)
+The Lost Sheep (Mt. 18:10-14, Lk. 15:3-7)
+The Unforgiving Servant (Mt. 18:23-35)
+The Good Samaritan (Lk. 10:29-37)
+The Friend at Midnight (Lk. 11:5-13)
+The Watchful Servants (Lk. 12:35-48)
+The Barren Fig Tree (Lk. 13:6-9)
+The Narrow Door (Lk. 13:22-30)
+The Great Banquet (Lk. 14:15-24)
+The Lost Coin (Lk. 15:8-10)
+The Prodigal Son (Lk. 15:11-32)
+The Unjust Steward (Lk. 16:1-15)
+Lazarus and the Rich Man (Lk. 16:17-31)
+The Unjust Judge (Lk. 18:1-8)
+The Pharisee and the Publican (Lk. 18:9-14)

Parables of Judgment *These parables emphasize a judgment (decision) must be made (by us!) whether or not to accept the inclusion/invitation (RSVP!). (Note that 2/3 of these parables occur in all three of the Synoptic Gospels.)*
+The Laborers in the Vineyard (Mt. 20:1-16; Mk. 10:31; Lk. 13:30)
+The Coins (Mt. 25:14-30; Mk. 13:34; Lk. 19:11-27)
+The Two Sons (Mt. 21:28-32)
+The Wicked Tenants (Mt. 21:33-46; Mk. 12:1-12; Lk. 20:9-19)
+The Wedding Banquet (Mt. 22:1-14; Lk. 14;15-24)
+The Fig Tree (Mt. 24:32-36; Mk. 13:28-32; Lk. 21:29-33)
+The Good and Wicked Slaves (Mt. 24:45-51; Lk. 12:41-46)
+The Ten Bridesmaids (Mt. 25:1-13)

Fascinating analysis of these may be found in Robert Farrar Capon's books, Parables of the Kingdom (1985), Parables of Grace (1988), and Parables of Judgment (1989), Eerdmans.

In Luke Alone

The narratives of Jesus' life exhibit tremendous parallels among the Gospels. Matthew, Mark, and Luke are called the "Synoptic Gospels" because of this similarity. However, Luke is unique in many aspects, with fully half of his Gospel account found only in his writing and not elsewhere. For example:

1:5-25   Zechariah's Encounter
1:26-38   Mary's Annunciation from Gabriel
1:39-56   Mary's Visitation with Elizabeth
1:57-80   Birth of John (the Baptist)
2:1-20   Jesus' Birth in Manger / Shepherds Heralded by Angels
2:21-24   Jesus' Presentation in the Temple
2:25-33   Simeon Recognizes Messiah
2:34-38   Anna Prophesies about the Child'
2:41-52   Jesus' Childhood Visit to Temple
6:24-26   Four Woes Follow Four Beatitudes
7:11-17   Raising a Widow's Son from the Dead
10:17-20   The Seventy Return
10:29-37   Parable about the Good Samaritan
10:38-42   Jesus Visits Mary and Martha
11:5-8   Parable about the Friend at Midnight
12:13-21   Parable about the Rich Fool
13:6-9   Parable about the Barren Fig Tree
13:10-17   Healing a Woman on the Sabbath
15:8-10   Parable about a Lost Coin
15:11-32   Parable about the Prodigal Son
16:1-12   Parable about the Unjust Manager
16:19-31   Parable about Lazarus and the Rich Man
17:11-19   Healing Ten Lepers
18:1-8   Parable about a Widow and an Unjust Judge
18:9-14   Parable about a Pharisee and a Tax Collector
19:1-10   Zacchaeus' Story
19:41-44   Jesus Laments over Jerusalem
24:13-35   Jesus' Appearance on the Road to Emmaus
24:50-53   Jesus' Ascension

(This list is by no means exhaustive.)

THE TRANSFIGURATION TEAM

Miraculous Parallels Prefiguring the Transfiguration

MOSES	ELIJAH	JESUS
Parted Red/Reed Sea	Parted Jordan River	Stilled stormy sea; Walked on water
*	*	*
Water/Manna for forty years	Refilling jars of oil & meal for widow	Feeding 5,000 with loaves & fishes
*	*	*
(Num. 21:4-9) Cured people of deadly serpent bites	Restored to life son of widow of Zarapheth	Restored to life son of widow of Nain
*	*	*
Buried by God-- No human knew where	Taken in chariot to heaven	Resurrection/ Ascension
*	*	*

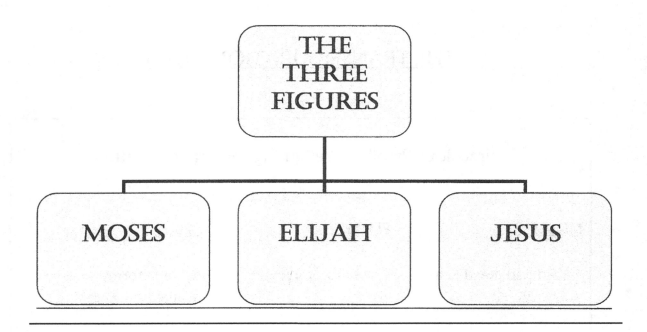

Why do you suppose these three figures configured the transfiguration?

MOSES	ELIJAH	JESUS
Exemplifies a Political Model	Exemplifies a Prophetic Model	Exemplifies a Priestly Model
of God's theme of Liberation	of God's theme of Restoration	of God's theme of Atonement
through Law	through Truth	through Sacrifice

THE ANOINTING STORIES in the NEW TESTAMENT

Source?	Who?	When?	Where?	With?	What Action?	Response?
Matthew 26:6-13						
Mark 14:3-9						
Luke 7:36-50						
John 12:1-8						

In the Old Testament, anointing was done in two circumstances:
(1)   Prophets anointed kings;
(2)   Bodies were anointed at death.

(Completed chart follows.)

THE ANOINTING STORIES

Source?	Who?	When?	Where?
Matthew 26:6-13	a woman	just prior to Last Supper	house of Simon (leper) in Bethany
Mark 14:3-9	a woman	just prior to Last Supper	house of Simon (leper) in Bethany
Luke 7:36-50	a sinful woman of the city	early in Jesus' ministry	house of a Pharisee
John 12:1-8	Mary of Bethany	six days prior to Passover	her own house in Bethany

In the Old Testament, anointing was done in two circumstances:
    (1)   Prophets anointed kings;
    (2)   Bodies were anointed at death.

(Left-hand side of chart)

in the NEW TESTAMENT

With?	What?	Response?
costly ointment in alabaster jar	Jesus' head	Disciples angry; Jesus—prep for burial
costly ointment in alabaster jar	Jesus' head	Disciples angry; Jesus—prep for burial
alabaster jar of ointment and her tears	Jesus' feet (and dried with her hair)	Pharisee said Jesus did know about her; Jesus—parable of forgiveness
pound of nard, costly perfume	Jesus' feet (and dried with her hair)	Judas—angry at waste Jesus—prep for burial

It was in the 4th century that St. Augustine erroneously deduced that it must have been Mary Magdalene in this story of anointing. Since then, the word "magdalene" has meant "prostitute"!

(Right-hand side of chart)

SEVEN SIGNS of JOHN'S GOSPEL

John's Gospel does not offer us "miracle" stories. Instead, he refers to "signs" which Jesus performed, seven of them specifically to show the glory of God. Now in the Old Testament, the glory of God always denoted the very presence of God. So, each of Jesus' signs gives us a glimpse of what Jesus' idea of life in the presence of God, which is to say abundant life, will look like.

Reference	Jesus' Sign	Old Testament Prophecy
John 2:1-11	**The Wedding at Cana**	Amos 9:13-14--a time to come in which "the mountains shall drip with sweet wine, and all the hills shall flow with it."
John 4:46-54	**Healing the Official's Son**	Ezekiel 34:16 says, "I will bind up the injured, and I will strengthen the weak."
John 5:1-9	**Healing the Lame Man**	Isaiah 35:6 states, "Then the lame shall leap like a deer."
John 6:1-14	**Feeding the Five Thousand**	Ezekiel 34:13 says, "I will feed them on the mountains of Israel."
John 6:16-21	**Calming the Stormy Sea**	Psalm 107 speaks of the LORD who controls the storm-tossed sea.
John 9	**The Man Born Blind**	Isaiah 35:5 states, "Then the eyes of the blind shall be opened."
John 11	**The Raising of Lazarus**	Ezekiel 37:13 states, "And you shall know that I am the LORD, when I open your graves, and bring you up from your graves, O my people."

SEVEN METAPHORS of JOHN'S GOSPEL

From the first chapter in John, when Jesus asks what people are looking for, everyone is trying to figure out who he is. Essentially, the rest of John's Gospel is the answer to that, as people come to their own conclusions about who Jesus is. John's Gospel is renowned for the seven great metaphors used by Jesus to describe himself. Interestingly, each of these have roots in Old Testament prophecy, which Jesus knew full well.

Reference	Jesus' Metaphor	Old Testament Prophecy
John 6:35	**I am the bread of life.**	Isaiah 55:10
John 8:12	**I am the light of the world.**	Isaiah 9:2
John 10:7	**I am the gate for the sheep.**	Jeremiah 23:3
John 10:11	**I am the good shepherd.**	Isaiah 40:11; Ezekiel 34:11-15
John 11:25	**I am the resurrection and the life.**	Isaiah 26:19
John 14:6	**I am the way, the truth, and the life.**	Much about walking in the holy way in Isaiah.
John 15:5	**I am the vine.**	Both Ezekiel and Zechariah are full of references to vines and vineyards.

Note: In addition to the seven metaphors, there are seven places in John's Gospel where John has Jesus proclaim, "I AM". Some translations render this as, "I am he," but that misses the point! When the Jews (or Judean authorities) heard Jesus saying, "I AM," they heard outright blasphemy; they heard Jesus claiming, "I AM God." (John 4:26; 6:20;8:24; 8:28; 8:58; 13:19; and 18:5,6,8) So, actually, when Thomas makes the statement in chapter 20, "My Lord and My God," he is proclaiming the punch-line for the entire Gospel. In fact, rather than the nick-name "Doubting Thomas", he should actually be remembered throughout history as "Proclaiming Thomas"!

JOHN'S GOSPEL PARALLELS between JESUS and GENESIS

The author of John's Gospel surely wishes us to recognize that Jesus has sovereignty over creation, in all of its facets. It is possible to find parallels in John's Gospel with the creation account.

Genesis	Gospel of John
Gen. 1:6-7 God separated the waters.	John 6:16-21 Jesus controls the stormy sea.
Gen. 1:14-18 God created light and separated light from darkness.	John 9:1-41 John restores sight (which is to say light!) to a man born blind.
Gen. 1:21-22 God created fish and told them to multiply.	John 6:2-13 When feeding 5,000 people, Jesus multiplied the fishes.
Gen. 2:7 God formed man from the dust of the ground.	John 9:6 Jesus mixes his saliva with dust from the ground to restore sight.
Gen. 2:8 God planted a garden and there he put the man.	John 18:1 Only in John's Gospel is Jesus arrested in a garden. (The other gospels name a place but do not call it a garden!) Jesus is also buried, and therefore resurrected, in a garden.
Gen. 2:7 God breathed the breath of life into the living being.	John 20:22 Jesus breathes on the disciples for them to receive the Holy Spirit.
Gen. 2:2-3 God hallows the seventh day creating the Sabbath.	John 5:10-17 Jesus reclaims the Sabbath for his true work.

JOHN'S GOSPEL PARALLELS between JESUS and MOSES

The story of the exodus and the wilderness sojourn was a defining time for the Israelites. It is possible to see parallels to the deeds of Moses in John's Gospel. Is this intentional? Seven such comparisons are:

Exodus	Gospel of John
Exodus 7:17-21 The water of the Nile is turned to blood, as a warning.	John 2:1-11 During a wedding, the water is turned to wine, as a blessing.
Exodus 14:21-31 The waters of the sea are driven back to allow the people to cross safely.	John 6:16-21 Jesus controls the stormy sea, saving his disciples.
Exodus 17:1-7 Moses struck the rock with his staff, and water gushed forth.	John 19:34 When Jesus' side is pierced by a spear, water and blood gush forth. (Jesus claims to offer Living Water.)
Exodus 16:2-26 Manna from heaven feeds the people in the wilderness.	John 6:2-14 Jesus, the Bread of Life, feeds 5,000 from a few barley loaves.
Numbers 21:5-9 Moses lifted up a bronze serpent on a pole, and viewing it would enable those who had been bitten by poisonous serpents to live.	John 3:14-15 Jesus says, "And just as Moses lifted up the serpent in the wilderness, so must the Son of Man be lifted up, that whoever believes in him may have eternal life."
Exodus 20 Moses gives God's Commandments to the people.	John 13:34 Jesus gives the new commandment that we love one another as he has loved us.
Moses was the guide to the Promised Land.	John 14:3 Jesus promises, "And if I go and prepare a place for you, I will come again and will take you to myself, so that where I am, you may be also." That's a *promised land!*

Outside of Johns' Gospel, other similarities are to be found, i.e.: Exodus 2—Pharaoh's order to drown Hebrew baby boys; Matt. 2:16—Herod's order to kill infants under two; Exodus 28:18—Moses was on the mountain 40 days; Mark 1:13—Jesus was in the wilderness 40 days.

A FULL CYCLE OF FEASTS

Internal Chronology in John's Gospel
--to Determine the Length of Jesus' Ministry

Chapter	Month	Jewish Date	Festival & Significance	John's Interpretation
2	Mar/Apr	15 Nisan	**Passover/Pesah**	Jesus begins his work; Temple is cleaned near the beginning in John, contrary to Matthew, Mark, and Luke.
		↕		
5	May/June	6 Sivan	A festival is mentioned that might be the spring barley harvest, which occurs 50 days after Pesah. It is **Shavuot**, **Pentecost**, or the **Festival of Weeks**.	Jesus feeds 5,000 with loaves of barley; Jesus claims he is the Bread of Life.
		↕		
6	*This chapter indicates "the Passover...was near"; but consider that this might not indicate the feast occurred. Jesus also speaks of the "last day" in this chapter, so it is likely that this is only a literary reference wherein John is looking ahead to what, for him, is the true and only Passover, Jesus' crucifixion.*			
7	September	15 Tishri	**Sukkot/Festival of Booths**, the autumn harvest ingathering, includes elaborate water rituals in the Temple, with prayers.	During the last day of this festival, Jesus enters the Temple and speaks of Living Water.
		↕		
10	December	25 Kislev	**Hanukkah/Festival of Lights** and **Temple Dedication**	Jesus claims to be the Light of the World; he restores sight to blind
		↕		
11-13	*References are again made to the approaching Passover. After all the repeated earlier statements that Jesus' hour was yet to come, we are now told that Jesus' hour had finally arrived.*			

Continues

19	Mar/Apr	14 Nisan	**Day of Preparation**, when a one-year-old unblemished lamb is prepared for Passover.	Unlike the Synoptic Gospels, John has the crucifixion occur on the Day of Prepara-tion and not on the Passover! Are we to think about the one-year-old un-blemished Passover lambs?
		↕		

20	*On the first day of the week after the Passover, Mary Magdalene finds the empty Tomb. A full year, and only one year, has been described in this Gospel.*

*Using this chronology, it is quite possible to contradict the prevailing notion that Jesus' ministry lasted three years. The Synoptic Gospels each compact Jesus' ministry into one year, so there is no reason to assume that John's Gospel, which uses a different sequence of events, as well, should be the sole source of determining that the ministry of Jesus' lasted three years, based upon its references to *Passover*. It is much more likely that John is using the word *Passover*, especially in chapter 6, as a metaphor of foretelling Jesus' death as the Lamb of God. (John is also the only Gospel that refers to Jesus as the Lamb of God. *John 1:29*)

Time Tension: Throughout the chapters of John, we find specific time references (such as "four o'clock in the afternoon", "forty-six years", or "two days"), details which indicate our human preoccupation with hour-by-hour and day-by-day earthbound time limitations (*chronos*). In contrast, this Gospel portrays Jesus not adhering to calendar or hour-glass constraints. Rather, he speaks metaphorically with a once-for-all-time, eternal approach to everything (*kairos*).

SEVEN LAST WORDS of CHRIST

Comparing the Gospel Viewpoints of the Passion Story

MARK

+38% of this Gospel centers on the Passion
+Addresses non-believers, to lead them to join the Gentile at the foot of the cross, to declare Jesus as true Son of God
+The narration is without embellishment
+Story-telling technique of Mark is evident:
  +3 prophecies of passion
  +3 times disciples fall asleep
  +3 times Peter denies Jesus
  +3 times Pilate appeals
+Jesus is mostly silent, but he speaks 3 times: before High Priest, before Pilate, and from the cross
+Jesus is in solitude and abandoned
+The only recognition is from a Gentile
+Last words are from Psalm 22, in which Jesus is beginning a recognized litany: "My God, my God, why have you forsaken me?"
+Concludes at an empty tomb (The verses after that are an editorial addition)

MATTHEW

+29% of this Gospel centers on the Passion
+Written to deepen faith and show the significance of Jesus
+Jesus, with authority as the Son of God, knows what will happen to him
+Shows Jesus "directing" events
+Adds the intervention of Pilate's wife
+Even the Romans recognize the righteousness of Jesus
+Shows the fulfillment of Scripture
+Jesus speaks the same last words as in Mark's narrative
+Only account to include an earthquake (upheaval)
+Grave is guarded

See next page for the information in Luke and John.

LUKE

+21% of this Gospel centers on the Passion
+Avoids distressing details, such as Judas' kiss or the scourging
+Notes that Jesus' blood is flowing in Gethsemane
+Has Jesus in "control"
>+Addresses and welcomes Judas gently
>+Heals the servant's sliced ear
>+Glances at Peter when the rooster crows
>+Speaks to the women
>+Speaks to the thief about Paradise
>+Forgives the executioners

+Proclaimed innocent 3 times by Pilate, as well as by the women, the thief, and the centurion
+Jesus does not drink the wine & myrrh
+Jesus is at peace and almost submissive
+Last words spoken:
>+"Father, forgive them..."
>+"Today you will be with me..."
>+"Father, into your hands..."

JOHN

+43% of this Gospel centers on the Passion
+There is no agony in Gethsemane
+Only John calls Gethsemane a garden
+"I AM" is repeated twice
+Jesus knows about and goes freely to his death
+The cross is a "lifting up"
+The cross is exaltation
+Jesus IS the Paschal Lamb
+The crucifixion is on a different day than the other three Gospels suggest
+Last words spoken:
>+"Woman, here is your son..."
>+"I am thirsty."
>+"It is finished."

+Jesus is laid in a garden.

PARALLELS in MINISTRY between LUKE and ACTS

The Gospel of Luke is the only one with a sequel, and that is the book of the Acts of the Apostles. Remarkable coincidences are evident, if one compares outlines of the two books, side-by-side. Are we meant to see that the followers of The Way are able to carry on the work of Jesus?

LUKE	ACTS
1:1-4 Dedication to Theophilus	1:1-5 Dedication to Theophilus
3:21-22 Holy Spirit descends upon Jesus	2:1-4 Holy Spirit fills the apostles
4:16-30 Jesus' sermon re: scripture's fulfillment	2:14-40 Peter's sermon re: scripture's fulfillment
5:17-25 Jesus heals a crippled man	3:1-10 Peter heals a crippled man
5:29-6:11 Conflicts with religious leaders	4:1-22 Conflicts with religious leaders
6:1-11 Conflict about Sabbath	5:17-42 Conflict with high priest
6:12-16 Jesus chooses 12 disciples	6:1-7 The 12 choose seven to serve
7:1-10 Story of the centurion's request	10:1-23 Story of the centurion's request
7:11-17 Jesus raises from the dead a widow's son	9:36-43 Peter raises from the dead a widow
9:28-35 Transfiguration—witnessed by Peter	10:9-16 Heavenly vision witnessed by Peter
9:51+ Jesus' face is set toward Jerusalem	19:21+ Paul resolves to go to Jerusalem
9:37 Jesus is joyfully welcomed in Jerusalem	21:17 Paul is welcomed warmly in Jerusalem

Continues

Continued

19:45 Jesus enters the Temple	21:26 Paul enters the Temple
20:27-39 Sadducees question Jesus	23:6-9 Council questions Paul
20:27 Sadducees do not believe in resurrection	21:8 Sadducees do not believe in resurrection
22:19 Jesus gives thanks and breaks bread	27:35 Paul gives thanks and breaks bread
22:54 Jesus is seized and led to the Council	21:30 Paul is seized and dragged to the Tribune
22:63-64 Jesus is struck	23:2 Paul is struck
22:66-23:13 Jesus appears four times before officials and is declared innocent three times	23:1-26:32 Paul is tried four times and declared innocent three times
23:18 Crowd shouts regarding Jesus: "Away with this fellow!"	21:36 Crowd shouts regarding Paul: "Away with him!"
23:47 Centurion speaks favorably about Jesus	27:43 Centurion wishes to save Paul
24:45-47 Scripture has been fulfilled	28:25-28 Scripture has been fulfilled

Support for this concept may be found in Fortress Introduction to the Gospels by Mark Allan Powell, Fortress Press, 1998, p. 88.

PROPHETIC VOCATION

Parallels between Calls of Paul and Jeremiah

Was Paul converted to Christianity, a word which did not even exist at that time? Or, was Paul ever faithful to Judaism, with his revelation being but a call to a new perception of Jesus as Messiah with himself as a prophet of this new perspective?

	JEREMIAH	PAUL
Predestiny	Jeremiah 1:5 "before you were born"	Gal. 1:15 "set me apart before I was born
Called by Voice of God	Jeremiah 1:1-9 "Now the word of the LORD came to me."	Acts 9:1-19, Gal. 1:1 "Paul an apostle sent neither by human commission nor from human authorities but through Jesus Christ and God the Father."
Ratifying Gesture	Jeremiah 1:9 "Then the LORD put out his hand and touched my mouth"	Acts 9:9 "For three days he was without sight, and neither ate nor drank."
Travel Instructions	Jeremiah 1:6 "for you shall go to all to whom I send you"	Acts 9:6 "But get up and enter the city and you will be told what you are to do."
Sent to Nations/ Gentiles	Jeremiah 1:10 "I appoint you over nations and over kingdoms."	Gal. 1:15 "that I might proclaim him among the Gentiles."
Word of God in Prophet's Mouth	Jeremiah 1:9 "Now I have put my words in your mouth."	II Corinthians 13:3 "Christ is speaking in me"
Sent to Proclaim	Jeremiah 1:7 "you shall go to all to whom I send you, and you shall speak whatever I command you."	Gal. 1:15 "God...was pleased to reveal his Son to me, so that I might proclaim him..."
Visions/ Revelations	Jeremiah 1:11-13; 24:1-10 visions of almond branches, boiling pots, good and bad figs.	II Corinthians 12:1-4 caught up into third heaven (likely Paul himself described)
Called Servant	Jeremiah 26:5 "heed the words of my servants the prophets whom I send to you"	Romans 1:1 "Paul, a slave of Jesus Christ, called to be an apostle."
Speech Problem	Jeremiah 1:6 "Truly I do not know how to speak..."	II Corinthians 10:10 "his bodily presence is weak and his speech is contemptible."
Suffers/Was Imprisoned	Jeremiah 32:2; 38:6	II Corinthians 11:23-33
Denounces Lies	Jeremiah 8:8; 9:5; 23:14	Romans 1:25; II Corinthians 6:11
Confronts False Prophets/Tchg.	Jeremiah 28:15 "Listen, Hananiah, the LORD has not sent you, and you made this people trust a lie."	II Corinthians 11:12-15 "I will also continue...to deny an opportunity to those who want... to be recognized as our equals in what they boast about. For such boasters are false apostles, deceitful workers."

Continued

Sends Others	Jeremiah 29:1 Letters sent	II Corinthians 8:16-24 Titus sent
Theme of Tearing Down and Building Up	Jeremiah 1:10	II Corinthians 10:8
Theme Against False Messages of Peace	Jeremiah 6:14	II Thessalonians 5:3
Theme of Potter and Clay	Jeremiah, chapters 18 & 19	Romans 9:20-24 II Corinthians 4:7-10
Theme of Concern for Poor	Jeremiah 22:16	Galatians 2:10 II Corinthians 8:13-15 II Corinthians 9:7
Theme of New Covenant	Jeremiah 31;31-34 "The days are surely coming, says the LORD, when I will make a new covenant with the House of Israel and the house of Judah. It will not be like the covenant that I made with their ancestors when I took them by the hand to bring them out of the land of Egypt—a covenant that they broke, though I was their husband, says the LORD. But this is the covenant that I will make with the house of Israel after those days, says the LORD: I will put my law within them, and I will write it on their hearts; and I will be their God, and they shall be my people."	II Corinthians 3:3-6 "and you show that you are a letter of Christ, prepared by us, written not with ink but with the Spirit of the living God, not on tablets of stone but on tablets of human hearts. ...Not that we are competent of ourselves to claim anything as coming from us; our competence is from God, who has made us competent ministers of a new covenant, not of letter but of spirit; for the letter kills, but the Spirit gives life."

ROLE of WOMEN in PAUL'S WORLD

Romans 16:1-6   Names ending in "-a" are feminine (i.e. Julia vs. Julius). In this passage, fully 1/3 of the names mentioned are women!

Galatians 3:28   This "baptismal formula" is considered the proof text for Paul's opinion of women.

MATER SYNAGOGAE / LEADER of HOUSE CHURCH Many tomb inscriptions support this title. (As house churches grew, they would combine into *ekklesia*.)
> **Mary** of Jerusalem, follower of John Mark (Acts 12:12)
> **Lydia** of Philippi, first convert in Europe (Acts 16:14-16,40)
> **Prisca/Priscilla** in Ephesus (Rom. 16:3-5; 1 Cor. 16:19)
> **Chloe** in Corinth (1 Cor. 1:11)
> **Nympha** in Laodicea (Col. 4:15)
> **Apphia** in Colossae (Philemon 1;2)

APOSTLE   One woman is called "apostle" by Paul. Unfortunately, from the 13th to the 20th centuries, translators changed her name to the masculine form, Junias, being unwilling to consider a woman in this role.
> **Junia** (Rom. 16:7)

DEACON   *Diakonia* is Greek for minister (source of our "deacon"). It is only applied to five people, four men: Paul, Apollos, Stephen, Philip, and this one woman. Unfortunately, until recently, as translators rendered this word describing her, they chose "servant" instead of "minister", possibly to diminish her apparent role of power.
> **Phoebe** (Rom. 16:1-2)

MISSIONARY   Usually missionaries were sent in pairs.
> **Four daughters** of Philip (Acts. 21:9 + writings of Eusebius)
> **Junia** & Andronicus (Rom.16:7)
> **Prisca** & Aquila (Same Prisca as above)

PREACHER-TEACHER-CO-WORKER   *Synergos* is the Greek word, which is only used for five people: Two men (Timothy and Titus) and three women:
> **Euodia** of Philippi (Phil. 4:2)
> **Synteche** of Philippi (Phil. 4:2)
> **Prisca** (Rom. 16:3)

THEOLOGIAN   The Greek verb for this is applied only three times in the New Testament; it is a word which means explaining the way of God. It is used for Peter (Acts 11:4), Paul (Acts 28:23) and the indefatigable:
> **Prisca** (Acts 18:26)

Dear Romans,

Paul shares his views with the Romans of his concepts of:

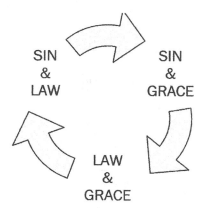

He concludes that in baptism we become dead to sin and alive to grace.

Tension still exists between two means of righteousness:

LAW > < GOSPEL

What the LAW could not do,   Christ has done, once and for all,

FREE US FROM SIN   FREED US FROM SIN.

Paving the way for

SANCTIFICATION

Sanctification is the work of the Holy Spirit. It is:
+ the power standing against sin;
+ the power to transform your life;
+ the power to present you as a "living sacrifice";
+ the power to attain "maturity, to the measure of the full stature of Christ" (Eph. 4:13)

According to Martin Luther, in his Large Catechism, sanctification is a process rather than an event. Creation is behind us, redemption has already occurred, but the Holy Spirit continues to work without ceasing to make us holy.

Blessed Be...

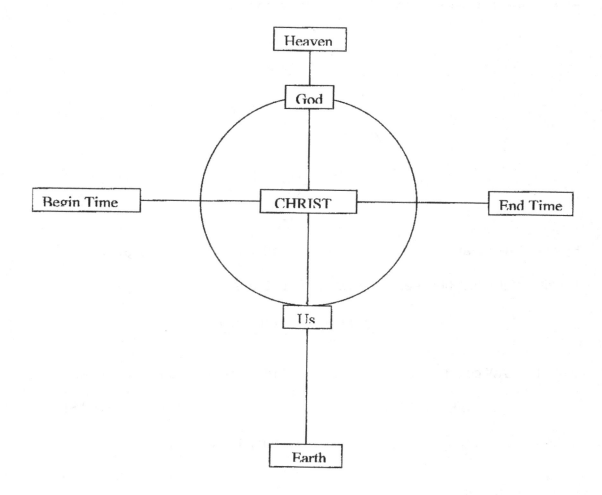

In the first chapter of Ephesians, following the salutation, is a beautiful benediction that is actually one long sentence in Greek, from verses 3 through 14! It is possible to envision this opening benediction of Ephesians within the diagram above. Paul writes of Christ gathering up in himself all things in heaven and earth. He writes of the fullness of time from before the foundation of the world. He writes of God's adoption of us as children, through Christ. The result: a "Celtic" cross.

THE APOCALYPTIC TENSE
Found in Revelation

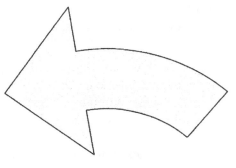

The author
takes an event
from the
PAST

To warn his
readers of
an existing
danger in the
PRESENT

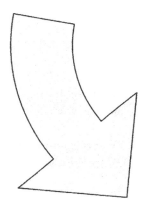

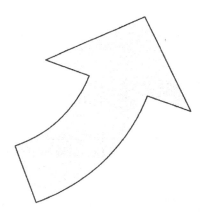

And he
predicts it
as an
event in
the FUTURE

The author of Revelation, John of Patmos, in the late 1st century AD, took an event from the past (the destruction of the Temple by the Babylonians), predicted it as a future "Coming Day of the Lord", to warn those of his generation of the evils of Roman persecution.

Some centuries earlier, the author of Daniel, in approximately the 2nd century BC, took an event from the past (the destruction of the Temple by the Babylonians), predicted it as a future "Coming Day of the Lord", to warn those of his generation of the evils of Antiochus Epiphanes, who had desecrated the Temple.

Note, the "Coming Day of the Lord' denotes movement, but it is not a calendar countdown toward destruction. Rather, it is always movement BY God toward his people, which is on-going and never-ending.

The THUNDERINGS of GOD

Threats or Theophanies?

Compare these Biblical examples of thunder associated with God. Is thunder a portent of punishment or a property of God's presence?

Ex. 19:16,19   On the morning of the third day there was **thunder** and lightning, as well as a thick cloud on the mountain, and a blast of a trumpet so loud that all the people who were in the camp trembled. As the blast of the trumpet grew louder, Moses would speak and God would answer him in **thunder**.

Job 37:2   Listen, listen to the **thunder** of his voice and the rumbling that comes from his mouth.

Job. 40:9   Have you an arm like God, and can you **thunder** with a voice like his?

Isa. 29:6   And in an instant, suddenly, you will be visited by the LORD of hosts with **thunder** and earthquake and great noise, with whirlwind and tempest, and the flame of a devouring fire.

Eze. 1:24   When they moved, I heard the sound of their wings like the sound of mighty waters, like the **thunder** of the Almighty.

John 12:28-29   Then a voice came from heaven, "I have glorified it, and I will glorify it again." The crowd standing there heard it and said that it was **thunder**.

Rev. 4:5   Coming from the throne are flashes of lightning, and rumblings and peals of **thunder**, and in front of the throne burn seven flaming torches, which are the seven spirits of God.

Rev. 6:1   Then I saw the Lamb open one of the seven seals, and I heard one of the four living creatures call out, as with a voice of **thunder**, "Come!"

Rev. 11:19   Then God's temple in heaven was opened, and the ark of his covenant was seen within his temple; and there were flashes of lightning, rumblings, peals of **thunder**, an earthquake, and heavy hail.

Rev. 14:2   And I heard a voice from heaven like the sound of many waters and like the sound of loud **thunder**; the voice I heard was like the sound of harpists playing on their harps.

Psalm 29:3,4,5,7,8,9   *Every reference in this psalm to the "voice of the LORD" is from a Hebrew word which may also be translated as thunder!*

POSTINGS from PATMOS FOLLOW a PATTERN

TEXT	CHURCH GREETED	DESCRIPTION of CHRIST	PRAISE/ REBUKE NARRATIVE	THE CHALLENGE	THE PROMISE/ FULFILLMENT	THE PROCLAMATION FORMULA
Rev. 2: 1-7	Ephesus					
Rev. 2: 8-11						
Rev. 2: 12-17						
Rev. 2: 18-29						
Rev. 3: 1-6						
Rev. 3: 7-13						
Rev. 3: 14-22						

(Completed in chart follows.)

📬 POSTINGS from PATMOS

TEXT in REVELATION	GREETING	DESCRIPTION of CHRIST, with references to the same ideas in the 1ˢᵗ chapter and the concluding chapters
	"To the angel of the church in _____, write…	"These are the words of _____ "
Rev. 2: 1-7	Ephesus	Holds 7 stars and stands among 7 lamps (Rev. 1:13,16 then Rev. 21:23)
Rev. 2: 8-11	Smyrna	The first & last; dead then alive (Rev. 1:17-18 then Rev. 22:13)
Rev. 2: 12-17	Pergamum	Has the two-edged sword (Rev. 1:16 then Rev. 19:15)
Rev. 2: 18-29	Thyatira	Son of God; eyes like flame; feet like bronze (Rev. 1:13-15 then Rev. 19:12)
Rev. 3: 1-6	Sardis	Has 7 spirits and 7 stars (Rev. 1:14,16)
Rev. 3: 7-13	Philadelphia	Holy one, true one, holds key (Rev. 1:18 then Rev. 22:16)
Rev. 3: 14-22	Laodicea	*The* Amen; faithful and true witness (Rev. 19:11; 22:21)

(Left-hand side of chart)

FOLLOW a PATTERN

PRAISE/ REBUKE NARRATIVE	CHALLENGE	PROMISE (Fulfillment)	PROCLAMATION FORMULA
"I know your…"		"To everyone who conquers…"	"Let anyone who has an ear listen to … the Spirit…"
Works, toil, & patient endurance	Repent!	Permission to eat from tree of life (Rev. 22:2,14)	Rev. 2:7
Affliction, poverty	Fear not; be faithful	Crown of life & no 2nd death (Rev. 20:6)	Rev. 2:11
Where you are living; food issue	Repent!	Hidden manna & new name on white stone (Rev. 22:4)	Rev. 2:17
Works—love, faith, service	Hold fast!	Morning star (Rev. 22:16)	Rev. 2:20
Works—dead not alive	Repent!	White robes, name in book of life (Rev. 20:12; 21:27)	Rev. 3:6
Works kept; open door	Hold fast!	Will be pillar in temple & have name written (Rev. 22:4)	Rev. 3:13
Works— lukewarm	Be earnest! Repent!	Place on the throne (Rev. 22:3)	Rev. 3:22

(Right-hand side of chart)

SERIOUS SERIES of SEVENS in REVELATION

The word/number **seven** is ubiquitous in Revelation! Specifically mentioned are:

Seven churches	**Seven** spirits	**Seven** golden lampstands
Seven stars	**Seven** seals on scroll	**Seven** horns
Seven eyes	**Seven** angels	**Seven** trumpets
Seven thunders	**Seven** heads	**Seven** diadems
Seven plagues	**Seven** golden bowls	**Seven** mountains

Sets of **seven** recur, as well, such as the **seven** cycles of visions, each with **seven** elements:

Cycle I.	Rev. 6:1-8—Scroll with **seven** seals
Cycle II.	Rev. 8:1-11:19—**Seven** angels with **seven** trumpets
CycleIII.	Rev. 12:1-13:18—**Seven** visions of conflict
Cycle IV.	Rev. 14:1-20—**Seven** visions of Mt. Zion
Cycle V.	Rev. 16:21—**Seven** bowls of wrath of God
Cycle VI.	Rev. 17:1-19:10—**Seven** visions of fall of Babylon
Cycle VII.	Rev. 19:11-21:5—**Seven** visions of victory

Seven "macarisms", or beatitudes, may be found throughout:

Rev. 1:3	Rev. 14:13	Rev. 16:15	Rev. 19:9
Rev. 20:6	Rev. 22:7	Rev. 22:14	

Seven references to the altar in heaven:

Rev. 6:9	Rev. 8:3	Rev. 8:5	Rev. 9:13
Rev. 11:1	Rev. 14:18	Rev. 16:7	

Seven statements about Jesus "coming soon":

Rev. 1:1	Rev. 2:16	Rev. 3:11	Rev. 22:6
Rev. 22:7	Rev. 22:12	Rev. 22:20	

Seven times "Babylon" is named (as code for "Rome"):

Rev. 14:8	Rev. 16:19	Rev. 17:5	Rev. 17:18
Rev. 18:2	Rev. 18:10	Rev. 18:21	

Seven times we find the four-fold inclusivity formula ("every tribe, language, people and nation"):

Rev. 5:9	Rev. 7:9	Rev. 10:11	Rev. 11:9
Rev. 13:7	Rev. 14:6	Rev. 17:15	

Seven times the "testimony" of Jesus is mentioned:

Rev. 1:2	Rev. 1:9	Rev. 12:17	Rev. 19:10
Rev. 19:10	Rev. 20:4	Rev. 22:16	

Seven times the "sword" of Jesus "mouth" is mentioned:

Rev. 1:16	Rev. 2:12	Rev. 2:16	Rev. 13:14
Rev. 19:15	Rev. 19:21 (twice)		

Seven times "this book" (i.e. The Revelation to John) is mentioned:

Rev. 1:11	Rev. 22:7	Rev. 22:9	Rev. 22:10
Rev. 22:18	Rev. 22:19 (twice)		

Seven times the "book of life" is named:

Rev. 3:5	Rev. 13:8	Rev. 17:8	Rev. 20:12
Rev. 20:12	Rev. 20:15	Rev. 21:27	

Many lists of things have seven-fold items in the listing:

Seven-fold praise in 5:11-12 (power, wealth, wisdom, might, honor, glory, blessing)

Seven calamities named in 6:12-14 (earthquakes, sun blackened, moon blood red, stars fall to earth, sky vanishes, mountains removed, islands removed)

Seven categories of those who wish to hide from the Lamb in 6:15 (kings of earth, magnates, generals, the rich, the powerful, slaves, free men)

Seven-fold praise in 7:12 (blessing, glory, wisdom, thanksgiving, honor, power, might)

Seven-fold description of the Lamb's protection in 7:15-17 (shelter, no hunger, no thirst, no sunburn, no scorching heat, guided to springs of water of life, all tears wiped away)

Compilation of a chart like this is made possible by use of a concordance. An excellent one is <u>The NRSV Concordance Unabridged</u> by John R. Kohlenberger, Zondervan, May 1991.

CYCLICAL SEVENS in REVELATION

SECTION in REVELATION	SYMBOL	REPRESENTS	IMAGE TAKEN FROM OLD TESTAMENT

[Chap. 4-5—Glimpse of heavenly worship!]

6:1-8 **SCROLL with SEVEN SEALS** (Worldly powers & death are limited.)

1–white horse	conquest	Zechariah 6:1-7
2–red horse	revolution	Zechariah 6:1-7
3–black horse	famine/economic disaster	Zechariah 6:1-7
4–pale green horse	pestilence	Zechariah 6:1-7
5–souls of martyrs	persecution	Zechariah 12:1-16
6–cosmic catastrophes	natural disasters	Joel 2:30-31; Isa.34:4;Hos. 10:8
7–silence		Job 4:16; Zech. 2:13

Interlude—Glimpse of worship!

8:1-11:19 **SEVEN ANGELS with SEVEN TRUMPETS** (Do not trust in created things.)

1–rain of fire, hail, blood; 1/3 earth destroyed	Exodus 9:23-35
2–mountain of fire into sea; 1/3 ships/sea creatures dead	Exodus 7:21
3–Wormwood falls into sea; 1/3 sea bitter	Jer. 9:15; 23:15
4–darkness; 1/3 sun, moon, stars dark	Ex. 10:21-22; Am. 8:9
5–hell opened—hordes of locusts	Ex. 10:12-15; Joel 1:4
6–monstrous cavalry; 1/3 humanity killed	Jer. 46:2-23

Interlude—Glimpse of worship!

7–God's temple is open

12:1-13:18 **SEVEN VISIONS OF CONFLICT** (Oppression of Church)

1–woman (Zion) in labor	
2–red dragon to devour child	Isa. 27:1; Daniel 7:1-8
3–Michael & angels battle dragon	Dan.10:13,21;Jude 1+
4–Satan thrown to earth	Luke 10:18
5–dragon attempts to overthrow	
6–beast from sea (Rome)	Daniel 7:2-3
7–beast from earth	Mt.24:24;2 Thes.2:9

14:1-20 **SEVEN VISIONS OF MT. ZION** (Reassurance amid persecution)

1–Lamb; 144,000; new song	Hebrews 12:22
2–eternal gospel announced	Psalm 19:1
3–fall of Babylon announced	Isa. 21:9;Dan. 4:30;Jer. 51:8
4–demise of beast's worshippers	Jer. 25:15-33; Ez. 38:22
5–blessing of dead (martyred)	
6–Son of Man harvests	Joel 3:13; Dan. 7:13-14
7–angel as vintner	Isaiah 63:34

Interlude—Glimpse of worship!

16:1-21	**SEVEN BOWLS OF WRATH OF GOD** (Remember how God delivered Israel from Egypt)	
	1—sores	Exodus 9:8-12
	2—sea into blood	Exodus 7:14-24
	3—rivers into blood	Exodus 7:14-24
	4—sun scorches	Isa. 49:10; Mt. 13:6
	5—kingdom of beast & darkness	Exodus 10:21
	6—Euphrates dries up; frogs	Nahum 1:4; Ex. 7:25-8:15
	7—earthquake & fall of Babylon (Rome)	Nah. 1:4; Jer. 51; Ex. 9:13

17:1-19:10	**SEVEN VISIONS OF FALL of BABYLON** (Fall of the oppressor)	
	1—judgment of whore	Isa. 23:17-18; Jer. 51:7
	2—mystery of heads & horns explained	Hos. 2:4 -5;Dan.7:7-8;11:2
	3—dirge for Babylon	Jer. 50-51; Ez. 26-27
	4—evacuation from doomed city	Jer. 51:45; Mt. 24:16
	5—millstone into the sea	Jer. 51:63
	6—destruction of Babylon	Jer. 51:63-64
	7—marriage of Lamb	Isa. 61:10
	*Interlude—**Glimpse of worship!***	

19:11- 21:5	**SEVEN VISIONS OF VICTORY**	
	1—rider on white horse/armies of heaven	Ez. 1:1; Isa. 11:4
	2—angel calls birds to prey on enemy	Ez. 39:4, 17-20
	3—beast & minions are defeated & killed	Dan. 7:11
	4—devil bound for 1,000 yrs.	2 Pet 2:4; Jude 1: 6
	5— thrones of judgment & souls of martyrs	Dan. 7:9,22; Mt. 19:28
	6—great white throne; books opened;	Dan. 7:10; Mt. 16:27;
	Death & Hades destroyed	Mt. 25:41; Rom. 2:6
	7—new heaven & new earth; holy city	Isa. 25:8; 35:10; 65:17; 66:22; Ez. 37:27; Rom. 8:18-21

Rev. 22:3-5—***Worship forever and ever!***

What can we take from these cycles? Look at the themes of what each cycle represents, and consider how often worship is emphasized.

Whom do you worship amidst worldly powers?
Whom do you worship amidst death?
Whom do you worship when created things fail?
Whom do you worship when the church is oppressed?
Whom do you worship amidst persecution?

In her book Revelation (Fortress Press, 1998), Elisabeth Schüssler-Fiorenza calls the interludes for worship the "Greek Chorus", punctuating the text!

Pouring Out Plagues

Plagues Delivered Upon Egypt	Seven Bowls of God's Wrath
Ex. 7:14-24 _____	Rev. 16:2 _____
Ex. 7:25-8:15 _____	Rev. 16:3 _____
Ex. 8:16-19 _____	Rev. 16:4 _____
Ex. 8:20-32 _____	Rev. 16:8 _____
Ex. 9:1-7 _____	Rev. 16:10 _____
Ex. 9:8-12 _____	Rev. 16:12 _____
Ex. 9:13-35 _____	Rev. 16:17 _____
Ex. 10:1-20 _____	
Ex. 10:21-29 _____	
Ex. 11:1-10 _____	

Find parallels in the two columns above.

The terminology of God's wrath in Revelation may be found in the Old Testament. The language is of theophany rather than punishment, illustrating the only power there is--is in God. Think of wrath, not as rage, but as in a reaction by the HOLY to anything unholy; it is deflected:

HOLY ⟲ UNHOLY

This blank chart is provided in order that classroom copies of the worksheet might be made. The completed chart is found on the following page.

Pouring Out Plagues

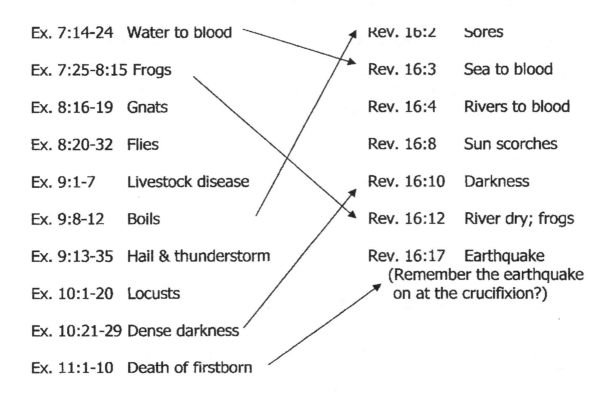

Ex. 7:14-24	Water to blood		Rev. 16:2	Sores
Ex. 7:25-8:15	Frogs		Rev. 16:3	Sea to blood
Ex. 8:16-19	Gnats		Rev. 16:4	Rivers to blood
Ex. 8:20-32	Flies		Rev. 16:8	Sun scorches
Ex. 9:1-7	Livestock disease		Rev. 16:10	Darkness
Ex. 9:8-12	Boils		Rev. 16:12	River dry; frogs
Ex. 9:13-35	Hail & thunderstorm		Rev. 16:17	Earthquake (Remember the earthquake on at the crucifixion?)
Ex. 10:1-20	Locusts			
Ex. 10:21-29	Dense darkness			
Ex. 11:1-10	Death of firstborn			

The terminology of God's wrath in Revelation may be found in the Old Testament. The language is of theophany rather than punishment, illustrating the only power there is--is in God. Think of wrath, not as rage, but as in a reaction by the HOLY to anything unholy; it is deflected:

HOLY ↶ UNHOLY

BEASTLY BEASTS
LITERARY or LITERAL?

SOURCE	DESCRIPTION	REPRESENTS
Revelation 13:1-3	Seven-headed, ten-horned leopard-like beast with bear-like feet and lion-like mouth	Rome (on its seven hills) and its emperors
Revelation 13:11-12	Two-horned beast	Priesthood of imperial cult
Daniel 7:4	Lion with wings of eagle	Babylonian Empire
Daniel 7:5	Bear with tusks	Median Empire
Daniel 7:6	Leopard with wings and 4 heads	Persian Empire
Daniel 7:7	Ten-horned beast	Alexander the Great's Empire
Job 40:15-24	Behemoth	Primeval creature of great strength
Job 41:1	Leviathan	Sea monster that personifies chaos
Psalm 74:14	Leviathan	Many-headed monster defeated by God as prelude to creation
Ancient Canaanite Myth	Twisting, many-headed serpent	Personified powers of chaos, evil, and destruction
Egyptian Myth	Behemoth (depicted as hippo) Leviation (depicted as crocodile)	Forces of chaos battled by the Egyptian deity Horus

Beauty and the Beast:
A Tale of Two Cities

The BEAST **Revelation 13--ROME**	**The BEAUTIFUL** **Revelation 21—NEW JERUSALEM**
Rising out of the sea— Rome dominates the Mediterranean Sea	Sea was no more— No more commerce
Having ten horns & seven heads— Rome sits on seven hills and had had 10 emperors	Coming down from heaven— God comes to dwell with us!
Ten diadems— Self-proclaimed emperors	Bejeweled city— Precious stones show true glory
Blasphemous names on heads— Emperors called themselves names like Savior or God Manifest	City is foursquare— Perfection represented by cube
Leopard-like, bear-like, & lion-like— Composite creature recalls Daniel's vision of Babylon, Persia, and Greece; but Rome is bigger than all these!	Twelve gates— Twelve tribes of Israel (Old Covenant)
	Twelve foundations— Twelve apostles (New Covenant)
Authority from dragon, i.e. Satan	No more tears— Death will be no more
Uttering blasphemies against God	No more sun or moon—light is God
Worshipped beast— Imperial cult	No Temple—Lord God Almighty and the Lamb reign
Made war on the saints— Persecutions	Nations & kings will come— Universal inclusivity
	Gates never shut— Open invitation

Excellent commentary about the Book of Revelation may be found in The Rapture Exposed by Barbara Rossing, WestView Press, 2005.

TYPES of LITERATURE within BIBLE

As an anthology, the Bible includes many books, written over a period of hundreds of years. Not only are there 66 different books listed in the contents, anyone who reads the Bible will notice the immense variety of literary styles between the covers. Some of those types include:

Prose and Poetry

Hymns and Prayers (Source of much liturgy)

Legal Codes and Genealogical Listings

Gospel (Form first exhibited by evangelist Mark)

Parables and Fables (Parable = narrative to illustrate a moral lesson; Fable = story to convey moral, especially with talking animals)

Proverbs and Allegories (Proverb = short, pithy saying embodying a general truth; Allegory = symbolic characters)

Biography and Autobiography (sections of Ezekiel & Revelation are auto-biographical)

Epistles and Sermons (Sermon = discourse, admonition, lecture, or reproof on moral or spiritual subject)

History and Etiological Myths (i.e. Tower of Babel narrative explains why there are so many different languages, so it is etiological)

Arguments and Diatribes (Diatribe = verbal attack or bitter criticism)

Dramas and Epics (Job's dialogue might be termed drama; Epic = extended story of heroic deeds, such as Samson's saga)

Oracles (a response of prophecy or advice)

Odes and Lyrics (Ode = lyric poem in an address, i.e. "To..."; Lyric = meant to be sung)

Idylls and Elegies (Song of Songs is an idyll; Psalm 137 is an elegy, i.e. song or poem of lament for the dead)

Dream Analysis (Joseph in Egypt, Daniel in Babylon)

Apocalypses (A revelation, of which very early examples may be found in Ezekiel)

UNFOLDING CHRONOLOGIES

Chronology of Each Creation Story

Genesis 1:1-2:3

God is named.

God created the **heavens** and earth.

1:2 **Spirit** of God (**Ruah**) swept over the waters.

Day One—Light

Day Two—Sky

Day Three—Earth & Vegetation

Day Four—Sun, moon, stars (to fill geography of 1st day)

Day Five—Swimming & flying creatures (to populate geography of 2nd day)

Day Six—Land creatures & humankind (to populate geography of 3rd day)

Day Seven—Rest

Genesis 2:4b-25

LORD God is named.

LORD God made the **earth** and the heavens.

2:7 **Breath** of life (**Ruah**) was breathed into his nostrils.

First—Adam from *adamah*, which is an "earthling" or creature from the earth

Second—Planted a garden (trees)

Third—Beasts of land and birds of sky

Fourth—Adam is split into man and woman, with the first use of gender-specific vocabulary.

This chart is a copy of that offered in the first chapter, since it is also useful as a chronology.

WOMEN of the BIBLE TIMELINE

CENTURY BC	TIME of	OUR LADIES
19th cent. BC	Patriarchs (@1887)	Sarah, Hagar, Rebekah, Rachel
18th cent. BC		
17th cent. BC	Sojourn in Egypt (1662)	
16th cent. BC		
15th cent. BC	Exodus (1447)	Miriam
14th cent. BC	Conquest of Canaan	
13th cent. BC	--time of Judges	Deborah, Jael, Delilah
12th cent. BC		Ruth, Hannah
11th cent. BC	United Kingdom (1053)	Bathsheba
10th cent. BC	Divided Kingdom (933)	Jezebel
9th cent. BC		Athaliah (842-836)
8th cent. BC	Fall of Samaria (721)	
7th cent. BC		
6th cent. BC	Fall of Jerusalem (588)	Esther
5th cent. BC	Babylonian Exile	
4th cent. BC	Greek rule	
3rd cent. BC		
2nd cent. BC	Seleucid rule	
1st cent. BC	Maccabees revolt	

1st cent. AD	Roman rule	Elizabeth, Mary, Mary & Martha, Mary Magdalene Sapphira, Lydia, Phoebe, Priscilla

PLOTTING the PROPHETS

Major Points of the Minor Prophets

The Twelve	Timeframe	Biography	Message/Theme
Jonah	Unknown, but Nineveh was destroyed in 612 BC	Son of Amittai	Forty Days More! Nineveh "Overturned"
Amos	760-745 BC (earliest); to Northern tribes	Sheepherder from Tekoa (5 mi. south of Bethlehem), but not a poor shepherd	Let Justice Roll Down! Introduces "Day of LORD" Surprisingly universalistic
Hosea	745-722 BC	Son of Beeri Lived in North Married harlot as metaphor	Unfaithful
722 BC—Fall of Samaria (Northern tribes) to Assyria			
Micah	720-701 BC to Northern tribes	From Moresheth (25 mi. SW of Jerusalem)	Walk Humbly Before God Three great principles in 6:8 summarize the law
Zephaniah	642-626 BC	Son of Cush	Day of LORD Is Near
Nahum	615-610 BC	Elkoshite	Fall of Lion's Den (Nineveh)
Habakkuk	611-605 BC	(contemporary to Jeremiah)	The Righteous Live by Faith
586 BC—Capture of Jerusalem by Babylonians			
Haggai	520 BC Post-exilic		Build My House! (Temple)
Zechariah	520-518 BC Post-exilic	Son of Berechiah	Return to Me! 8 visions of community center on Temple for security
520-515 BC—Temple is rebuilt			
Obadiah			God's Justice
Joel	516 BC Post-exilic	Son of Pethuel	Day of LORD Is Coming
Malachi	anywhere from 516 to 330 BC		Prepare the Way Before Me

Very helpful information about these books may be found in The Literary Structures of the Old Testament *by David A. Dorsey, Baker Books, 1999.*

A FULL CYCLE OF FEASTS

Internal Chronology in John's Gospel
--to Determine the Length of Jesus' Ministry

Chapter	Month	Jewish Date	Festival & Significance	John's Interpretation
2	Mar/Apr	15 Nisan	**Passover/Pesah**	Jesus begins his work; Temple is cleaned near the beginning in John, contrary to Matthew, Mark, and Luke.
		↕		
5	May/June	6 Sivan	A festival is mentioned that might be the spring barley harvest, which occurs 50 days after Pesah. It is **Shavuot**, **Pentecost**, or the **Festival of Weeks**.	Jesus feeds 5,000 with loaves of barley; Jesus claims he is the Bread of Life.
		↕		
6	*This chapter indicates "the Passover...was near"; but consider that this might not indicate the feast occurred. Jesus also speaks of the "last day" in this chapter, so it is likely that this is only a literary reference wherein John is looking ahead to what, for him, is the true and only Passover, Jesus' crucifixion.**			
7	September	15 Tishri	**Sukkot/Festival of Booths**, the autumn harvest in-gathering, includes elaborate water rituals in the Temple, with prayers.	During the last day of this festival, Jesus enters the Temple and speaks of Living Water.
		↕		
10	December	25 Kislev	**Hanukkah/Festival of Lights** and **Temple Dedication**	Jesus claims to be the Light of the World; he restores sight to blind
		↕		
11-13	*References are again made to the approaching Passover. After all the repeated earlier statements that Jesus' hour was yet to come, we are now told that Jesus' hour had finally arrived.*			

Continues

19	Mar/Apr	14 Nisan	**Day of Preparation**, when a one-year-old unblemished lamb is prepared for Passover.	Unlike the Synoptic Gospels, John has the crucifixion occur on the Day of Prepara-tion and not on the Passover! Are we to think about the one-year-old un-blemished Passover lambs?

20   *On the first day of the week after the Passover, Mary Magdalene finds the empty Tomb. A full year, and only one year, has been described in this Gospel.*

*Using this chronology, it is quite possible to contradict the prevailing notion that Jesus' ministry lasted three years. The Synoptic Gospels each compact Jesus' ministry into one year, so there is no reason to assume that John's Gospel, which uses a different sequence of events, as well, should be the sole source of determining that the ministry of Jesus' lasted three years, based upon its references to *Passover*. It is much more likely that John is using the word *Passover*, especially in chapter 6, as a metaphor of foretelling Jesus' death as the Lamb of God. (John is also the only Gospel that refers to Jesus as the Lamb of God. *John 1:29*)

Time Tension: Throughout the chapters of John, we find specific time references (such as "four o'clock in the afternoon", "forty-six years", or "two days"), details which indicate our human preoccupation with hour-by-hour and day-by-day earthbound time limitations (*chronos*). In contrast, this Gospel portrays Jesus not adhering to calendar or hour-glass constraints. Rather, he speaks metaphorically with a once-for-all-time, eternal approach to everything (*kairos*).

APOCALYPTIC TENSE

A literary "tense" with aspects of three tenses at the same time. (Curiously, the name YHWH also has aspects of three tenses at the same time!)

PAST   **PRESENT**   **FUTURE**

$+$

The writer

Takes an event from
the past

◀┅

Predicting it as a future event

┅▶

To warn of a current evil

◀┅

$+$

Example One: The author of Daniel, in approximately the 2ⁿᵈ century BC, took an event from the past (the destruction of the Temple by the Babylonians), predicted it as a future "Coming Day of the Lord", to warn those of his generation of the evils of Antiochus Epiphanes, who had desecrated the Temple.

Example Two: The author, John of Patmos, in the late 1ˢᵗ century AD, took an event from the past (again, the destruction of the Temple by the Babylonians), predicted it as a future "Coming Day of the Lord", to warn those of his generation of the evils of Roman persecution.

Note: The "Coming Day of the Lord" denotes movement, but it is not a calendar countdown toward destruction, rather it is always movement BY God toward his people, which is ongoing and never-ending.

✡   PATTERNS in WORSHIP   ☦

Israelites in the Wilderness

(Exodus, ch. 19-25)
People purify themselves
People assemble
Word of LORD is spoken
Message given (instruction,
          admonition, exhortation)
Elders & priests process
Covenant is read
Blood of the covenant ceremony
Offerings received

Second Temple

(Nehemiah, ch. 9)
People, having fasted, assemble
Confession of sins
Torah readings
Confession
Praises to God
Message given
Pledge of renewal to covenant

Early Church (150 A.D.)

(According to Roman historian, Justin)
Readings from prophets & apostles
Psalm sung
Sermon
Intercessory prayers
Kiss of peace
Bread & wine offered
Thanksgiving prayer
"Amen" response
Distribution of bread & wine
Offering for needy

Medieval Mass

   Liturgy of the Word
Introit/Entrance
Kyrie/Lord have mercy
Confession & forgiveness
Gloria/Glory to you...
Dominus vobiscum/Lord be with you
Collects (prayers)
Epistle reading
Alleluia/Gradual for season
Gospel reading
Creed
   Eucharistic Feast
Offertory
Sursum corda/Lift up your hearts
Sanctus/Holy, holy, holy
Benedictus/Blessed are you...
Canon of the Mass
Lord's Prayer
Agnus Dei/Lamb of God
Communion
Ite, missa est. Deo gratias./
      Go. It is the sending
      Thanks be to God.

TIMELINE FOR BIBLICAL TRANSLATIONS

The OT was written primarily in Hebrew. A couple of sections were written in Aramaic. We know Aramaic as the language spoken by Jesus, but it was the language the people acquired during their Babylonian Captivity and Exile. They brought it back to Judea with them, when the Persians allowed them to return home. From then on, Hebrew was used primarily for liturgical purposes! The NT was written in Greek.

500 BC   Much of the **Torah** had been translated into Aramaic.

250 BC   **Septuagint**—this is the Latin word for 70; sometimes it is abbr. LXX. *Written in Alexandria, this is the first translation into Greek of the Hebrew Bible. A Greek translation was needed, because more Jews lived in Greek-speaking cities than in Palestine! Legend claims that 70 scribes worked independently for 70 days, and each translation, thanks to divine inspiration, was identical! The Septuagint is the Bible of Jesus' day. Whenever the OT was quoted in the NT, it was from the Septuagint.*

325 AD   **Codex Vaticanus**--This is a trustworthy copy of both OT & NT in Greek. *This text, which has been residing in the Vatican's library since 1480, was written on* **vellum**, *which is treated animal hide.*

350 AD   **Codex Sinaiticus**
This text, written on sheep and goatskin parchment, was discovered at St. Catherine's Monastery at the foot of Mt. Sinai in the 19th cent.

390-405   **Vulgate**--St. Jerome's translation of the Septuagint into Latin.
It is called the Vulgate, meaning "common", because the people primarily spoke Latin. Jerome said of his translation that "any other version was a subversion!"

When Charlemagne was in power (768-814 AD), he ordered churches to read the Vulgate in dialects which the people could understand. Over the centuries, as dialects evolved, eventually most people could no longer understand Latin, as the Romance languages became standardized, which is how it came to pass that the mass was being spoken in Latin until late in the last century, and most folks could not understand it! In any event, it is the Vulgate that missionaries from Rome took to England.

Continues

7th cent.   **Masoretic Text**

*In Hebrew only the consonants were written. A group of scholars, called **Massoretes**, added the points for the vowel sounds, above the consonants. This text became the standard for the OT until the mid-1900's. The Massoretes were meticulous scribes; they would count every letter of each copy to be sure it was identical to the original being used, to help insure no errors were occurring.*

8th cent.   Bede translated the *gospels* into English; he finished John on his deathbed!

9th cent.   A partial translation into Anglo-Saxon (Olde English) was made.

10th cent.   English King Alfred the Great translated the Ten Commandments and the Psalms into English.

10th cent.   **Lindisfarne Gospels**—the earliest English NT

The Irish monasteries were producing illuminated manuscripts.

1226   **Stephen Langton**, Archbishop of Canterbury, added the chapter numbers.

1329-1384   **John Wycliff**, a contemporary of Chaucer and an Oxford theologian, made the first complete and full English translation from the Latin. He was "reproved" by the Pope, but he survived. Decades after his death, he was condemned for heresy, so his body was dug up and burned!

1453   **Gutenberg Press**

1522   **Martin Luther** began his translation of the NT into the German tongue.

1534   Publication of full German translation of entire Bible

In the next 40 years, over 100,000 copies were sold, so that virtually every German home had a copy. Luther even printed large print Bibles for those with poor eyesight!

1525   **William Tyndale** completed an English translation of the NT from Greek.

1535   **Myles Coverdale**, influenced by Luther, completed Tyndale's work.

1537   Henry VIII, having broken with the Pope, gave royal approval to Coverdale's English translation.

1543   Parliament prohibited the use of English translations, making it a crime for any unlicensed person to read or explain Scripture in public. Copies were burned.

Continues

1551   A Parisian printer added the verse numbers.

1560   **Geneva Bible**, another English translation—popular due to its small size and moderate price, especially among English people exiled in Geneva
It was banned in England. It is sometimes called the "Breeches" Bible, because it translated Gen. 3:7 as "They sewed fig leaves together and made themselves breeches."

1607   **King James Bible**, at the command of King James I, contemporary to William Shakespeare, 50 scholars, divided into companies, were appointed to write this translation.*

1632   **Bishops' Bible**, called the "Wicked Bible", because it left out the word "not" in the 7th commandment, leaving this: "Thou shalt commit adultery."

1946   **Revised Standard Version**
Considered a "literal" translation, this Bible attempted to use idioms without using paraphrasing.

1947-1948 **Dead Sea Scrolls** discovered.
The fragments, when reconstructed, show portions of every book of our Bible, except Esther. The copies have been dated to between 100 BC and 100 AD and were made at Qumran, a community of ascetic Jews. They are 1,000 years older than the Masoretic texts, but astoundingly there is very little difference between them, so the scribes had worked with extreme care..

1952   **New Revised Standard Version**
The NRSV reflects continued archaeological discoveries, plus its vocabulary removes gender bias. It is considered "literal, with the freedom to be idiomatic".

1962, 1966 **The Living Bible**
An interpretive paraphrase, meant to share the message of God in the common vernacular.

1966, 1976 **The Good News Bible**
It does not conform to traditional style or vocabulary but hopes to express meaning in the manner people speak today.

An excellent resource for information about the King James Version is in Adam Nicolson's God's Secretaries, Harper Collins.

TIMELINE FOR NEW TESTAMENT WRITING & CANONIZING

All dates are AD (Anno Domini) or CE (Common Era):

36	Paul's conversion experience
51-63	Paul's letter writing years
68	Mark's gospel (teaching of Peter, written in Rome?)
75-85	Luke's gospel (to Gentiles, written in Antioch?)
75-85	Matthew's gospel (to former Jews, written in Syria Palestine)
90	John's gospel (written as catechism in Ephesus?)
95	John of Patmos wrote his apocalypse (Revelation)

1st cent.   Historian Josephus refers to 22 books of the Bible (i.e. NT).

160   Irenaeus (early church father—student of Polycarp, who was student of John the Evangelist!)—identified a four gospel canon, which he called the *Tetramorph*.

200's   Origen of Alexandria was using the same 27 books found in today's NT, but there were still disputes over Hebrews, James, II Peter, II & III John, and Revelation.
Origen also offered a sequential reading list for the educated Christian to follow. First, would be Esther, Judith, Tobit, and Wisdom; second would be the Gospels, the Epistles, and the Psalms; and, third would be Leviticus and Numbers!

367   Athanasius, Bishop of Alexandria, in an Easter letter, listed books which match our NT. He used the phrase ***kanonizomena*** = "being canonized". In his OT list, he excluded Esther but included the Book of Baruch and a Letter of Jeremiah.

393   Council of Carthage & African Synod of Hippo, led by St. Augustine, approved the NT, as it stands today and called the canon closed. As for the OT, any books included in the **Septuagint** were chosen.

1546 Church.   Council of Trent makes a statement of the canon for the Catholic Church.

1563   Church of England's "Thirty-Nine Articles of 1563" identifies its canon.

1647   Westminster Confession of Faith accepts the canon for Calvinism.

1672   Synod of Jerusalem accepts the canon for the Greek Orthodox.

UNIQUE
CROSSWORDS

GENESIS

The first book of the Bible, Genesis, is full of characters more flawed than a soap opera. The book opens with the first murder, but it does end on a grace note of forgiveness. Using the clues from the NRSV translation, fill in the blanks. Then take the boxed letter from each word to fill in the blanks below for a message, which is a running theme of Genesis.

1. The mother of Ishmael, cast out by Sarah, was _ _ ☐ _ _. (21:9-10)
2. God determined to destroy all life, because the earth was _ ☐ _ _ _ _ _. (6:11)
3. Cain committed the first _ _ _ ☐ _ _. (4:8)
4. Worried that Pharaoh would kill him, Abram claimed Sarai was his _ ☐ _ _ _ _. (12:13)
5. As Noah lay drunk in his _ _ ☐ _, his son saw him. (9:21)
6. Eve told God the _ _ _ _ _ ☐ tricked her. (3:13)
7. Sarah dealt harshly with her _ _ _ _ ☐ _ _ _ _ when a child was conceived. (16:6)
8. At the grave sin of Sodom and Gomorrah, the LORD sent two _ ☐ _ _ _ _ to investigate. (19:15)
9. Laban tricked Jacob by switching his ☐ _ _ _ _ _ _ _ on the wedding night. (29:16-30)
10. Joseph's brothers sold him to Ishmaelites for 20 pieces of _ _ _ _ ☐ _. (37:28)
11. Laban attempted to cheat Jacob by moving the best livestock the ☐ _ _ _ _ _ _ _ of a three days' journey. (30:25-43)
12. Rebekah tricked Isaac when she covered Jacob's hands and neck with _ _ ☐ _ _ of goats. (27:16)
13. Was Tamar's pregnancy a _ _ _ _ _ ☐ of prostitution with her father-in-law? (38:24)
14. The offspring of Lot and his ☐ _ _ _ _ _ _ _ _ daughter was the ancestor of the Moabites. (19:36-38)
15. Joseph's brothers hated him, especially when his father gave him a _ ☐ _ _. (37:3-4)
16. Rachel lied about why she could not ☐ _ _ _ from her camel's saddle. (31:34)
17. Because she had Joseph's ☐ _ _ _ _ _ _, Potiphar's wife's lie was believed. (39:7-18)
18. The people of Shinar, desiring a name for themselves, built a _ ☐ _ _ _ to reach the heavens. (11:1-9)
19. Knowing that God intends all for good, Joseph was able to _ ☐ _ _ _ _ _ his brothers. (50:15-21)
20. Joseph's brothers were worried that Joseph might still bear a _ _ _ ☐ _ _ against them for selling him into slavery. (50:15)

☐ ☐ ☐   ☐ ☐ ☐ ☐ ☐ ☐ ☐

☐ ☐   ☐ ☐ ☐   ☐ ☐ ☐ ☐

Answer Key for **GENESIS**

HA<u>G</u>AR
C<u>O</u>RRUPT
MUR<u>D</u>ER
S<u>I</u>STER
TE<u>N</u>T
SERPEN<u>T</u>
SLAV<u>E</u>GIRL
A<u>N</u>GELS
<u>D</u>AUGHTERS
SIL<u>V</u>ER
<u>D</u>ISTANCE
SK<u>I</u>NS
RESUL<u>T</u>
<u>F</u>IRSTBORN
R<u>O</u>BE
<u>R</u>ISE
<u>G</u>ARMENT
T<u>O</u>WER
F<u>O</u>RGIVE
GRU<u>D</u>GE

GOD INTENDED IT FOR GOOD

EXODUS

Using clues from the NRSV translation, fill in the blanks. The letters in the boxes should then be placed in the spaces below to discover something you should have learned in catechism class.

1. God establishes this (19:5)   ☐ _ _ _ _ _ _ _

2. A hard-hearted one (7:13)   _ _ _ _ _ ☐ _

3. He saw God (33:22-23)   ☐ _ _ _ _

4. What is it? (16:31)   ☐ _ _ _ _

5. Mighty acts of God (8:2)   _ _ ☐ _ _ _ _

6. Miriam's response to deliverance (15:21)   _ _ ☐ _

7. People pledge this to God (24:7)   _ _ _ ☐ _ _ _ _ _

8. Forty days and nights atop (24:15-18)   ☐ _ _ _ _   _ _ _ _ _

9. Aaron was ordained as the first (28:1)   _ _ _ ☐ _ _

10. Abode of the LORD (40:34-38)   _ _ _ _ _ ☐ _ _ _ _

11. New sign of the covenant (31:12-17)   _ _ _ _ _ ☐ _

12. Saved by the blood of a lamb (12:27)   _ _ _ ☐ _ _ _ _

☐ ☐ ☐ ☐ ☐ ☐ ☐ ☐ ☐ ☐ ☐ ☐

Answer Key for **EXODUS**

<u>C</u>OVENANT
PHARA<u>O</u>H
<u>M</u>OSES
<u>M</u>ANNA
PL<u>A</u>GUES
SO<u>N</u>G
OBE<u>D</u>IENCE
<u>M</u>OUNT SINAI
PRI<u>E</u>ST
TABER<u>N</u>ACLE
SABBA<u>T</u>H
PAS<u>S</u>OVER

COMMANDMENTS

NUMBERS

This complex book follows the people on their journey from Sinai to the Transjordan. Using the NRSV translation, fill in the blanks for each clue. Then take the boxed letters to fill in the spaces at the bottom to discover the Hebrew name for this book.

1. The LORD gave Moses instructions for making and using two _ ☐ _ _ _ _ trumpets. (10:1-10)
2. In the story of Balaam, there is a talking _ _ ☐ _ _ _. (Ch. 22)
3. Once when the people complained, the LORD sent _ _ _ _ _ _ ☐ _ that killed them, but Moses was instructed to make one of bronze to use as a cure. (21:6-9)
4. When _ _ _ _ _ ☐ _ _ _ _ died with no sons, his daughters were allowed to keep possession of the inheritance. (27:1-11)
5. Numbers opens with the LORD's command for Moses to take a _ ☐ _ _ _ _; a second one was required before entry into the promised land. (1:2; 26:2)
6. Moses reminded the LORD of his promise, saying, "The LORD is _ _ _ ☐ to anger, and abounding in steadfast love, forgiving iniquity and transgression." (14:18)
7. When Moses' sister and brother spoke against his marrying a Cushite woman, the LORD became angry and left _ ☐ _ _ _ _ leprous for seven days. (12:1-15)
8. The people complained and craved meat, so the LORD brought them _ _ _ _ ☐ but then sent a plague which killed them while the meat was still between their teeth. (Ch. 11)
9. The selection of Aaron as priest was affirmed when the LORD caused his staff alone to produce _ _ _ _ _ ☐ _. (17:1-11)
10. The LORD ordered spies to be sent into Canaan for 40 days, but when Joshua and _ _ _ ☐ _ returned and gave their advice to trust the LORD, the people threatened to stone them. (13:1 – 14:19)
11. After Korah's rebellion, the _ _ ☐ _ _ opened its mouth and swallowed the rebels and their households. (16:1-32)
12. Numbers opens in the wilderness of _ _ ☐ _ _, just two years after the exodus from Egypt. (1:1)
13. Many rituals are described in this book, but one purification rite required the offering of a _ ☐ _ heifer without blemish. (19:1-3)
14. The LORD gave instructions for Aaron to _ _ _ ☐ _ the Israelites with these words: "The LORD _ _ _ _ _ you and keep you; the LORD make his face to shine upon you, and be gracious to you; the LORD lift up his countenance upon you, and give you peace." (6:22-27)
15. When the cloud of the LORD covered the tabernacle, the people remained encamped, but when it lifted, the people were to break camp and set out until the cloud ☐ _ _ _ _ _ _ down again. (9:15-23)

☐☐ ☐☐☐ ☐☐☐☐☐☐☐☐☐☐

Answer Key for **NUMBERS**

S<u>I</u>LVER
DO<u>N</u>KEY
SERPEN<u>T</u>S
ZELOP<u>H</u>EDAD
C<u>E</u>NSUS
SLO<u>W</u>
M<u>I</u>RIAM
QUA<u>I</u>L
ALMON<u>D</u>S
CAL<u>E</u>B
EA<u>R</u>TH
SI<u>N</u>AI
R<u>E</u>D
BLE<u>S</u>S
<u>S</u>ETTLED

IN THE WILDERNESS

112

JOSHUA

Find the answer to each clue, then use the designated letter from each word to fill in the empty squares below, in order. You will discover to whom Canaan (the Promised Land) was allotted as an inheritance. References are from the NRSV.

1. The book which precedes Joshua is _ _ _ ❑ _ _ _ _ _ _ _ .
2. There were _ ❑ _ _ _ stones taken from the river and set up at Gilgal as a memorial to the crossing. (4:19-24)
3. Upon the death of _ _ _ ❑ _, the LORD spoke to Joshua about becoming the leader. (1:1)
4. The ancestors of the Israelites had been promised a land flowing with _ _ ❑ _ and honey. (5:6)
5. Joshua made a _ _ ❑ _ _ _ _ with the people, when they affirmed they would serve the LORD alone. (24:24-25)
6. In the conquest of the city _ _ _ ❑ _ _, the LORD caused the sun and the moon to stand still. (10:12-13)
7. The tribe of Levi alone received no _ _ _ _ _ _ ❑ _ _ _ _ of land. (13:14)
8. The river dramatically crossed to enter Canaan was the _ _ ❑ _ _ _. (Ch. 3)
9. During the conquest of Canaan, _ _ _ ❑ _ _ _ was the first city to be utterly destroyed while obeying the LORD's orders. (Ch. 6)
10. The woman who hid the two spies was _ _ _ _ ❑. (Ch. 2)
11. The number of priests and trumpets and days in the procession of the Ark of the Covenant around Jericho was _ _ _ ❑ _. (6:3-4)
12. The book which follows Joshua in the Old Testament is _ _ _ _ _ ❑.

❑ ❑ ❑ ❑ ❑ ❑

❑ ❑ ❑ ❑ ❑

Answer Key for **JOSHUA**

DEU<u>T</u>ERONOMY
T<u>WE</u>LVE
MOS<u>E</u>S
MI<u>L</u>K
CO<u>V</u>ENANT
GIB<u>E</u>ON
INHERI<u>T</u>ANCE
JO<u>R</u>DAN
JER<u>I</u>CHO
RAHA<u>B</u>
SEV<u>E</u>N
JUDG<u>E</u>S

TWELVE TRIBES

JUDGES

The events described in this book follow a cyclical pattern which begins with the Israelites doing the thing named in the boxes below again and again. First, find the words to answer each clue (NRSV translation). Then use the indicated letter of the clue word to fill in the empty spaces below.

1. _ _ _ ❑ _ _ killed 1,000 Philistines with the jawbone of a donkey. (15:14-17)
2. The book of Judges follows the book and death of _ ❑ _ _ _ _.
3. Deborah's _ ❑ _ _ of deliverance is the oldest part of our Bible. (Ch. 5)
4. Whenever the Israelites forgot God and worshipped idols, the _ ❑ _ _ _ of the LORD was kindled. (2:12; 2:20; 3:8;10:7)
5. A particularly shocking story is the rape and murder of the concubine belonging to the _ _ _ _ ❑ _. (19:1-30)
6. The nagging woman who discovered the secret for Samson's strength was named _ _ _ _ _ _ ❑. (16:4-22)
7. Whenever the LORD raised up a judge, he delivered the Israelites from the hand of their _ _ ❑ _ _ _ _. (2:18)
8. The Israelites are frequently reminded that the LORD brought them up from the land of _ _ ❑ _ _. (2:12; 6:8; 6:13; 10:11)
9. _ _ _ _ ❑ _ _ _ foolishly promised a burnt offering to the LORD for victory over the Ammonites. (11:29-33)
10. Jephthah's offering to the LORD turned out to be his own _ _ ❑ _ _ _ _ _. (11:34-40)
11. The book of Judges concludes with the thematic problem restated, "In those days there was no king in Israel; all the people did what was ❑ _ _ _ _ in their own eyes." (21:25)
12. In those days there was no _ _ ❑ _ in Israel. (18:1; 19:1; 21:25)
13. In Judges, the pattern of apostasy begins with the statement, "Then the Israelites did what was ❑ _ _ _ in the sight of the LORD." (2:11; 3:7; 3:12; 4:1; 6:1; 10:6; 13:1)
14. A left-handed person named _ _ _ ❑ killed a fat king. (3:12-30)
15. The murder of Sisera by _ ❑ _ _ delivered the Israelites from him. (4:17-22)
16. Whenever a judge died, the people would _ _ _ _ _ ❑ _ and behave worse. (2:19)
17. Whenever the LORD raised up a judge, he _ _ _ ❑ _ _ _ _ _ them from the hand of their enemies. (2:18)
18. _ _ ❑ _ _ _ selected his troops for an attack on the Midianites based upon how they drank water. (Ch. 6-7)
19. The female judge _ ❑ _ _ _ _ _ accompanied Barak to defeat the Canaanites. (Ch. 4)

❑❑❑❑ ❑❑❑❑ ❑❑❑❑❑ ❑❑❑❑❑.

Answer Key for **JUDGES**

SAM<u>S</u>ON
J<u>O</u>SHUA
S<u>O</u>NG
A<u>N</u>GER
LEVI<u>T</u>E
DELILA<u>H</u>
EN<u>E</u>MIES
EG<u>Y</u>PT
JEPH<u>T</u>HAH
DA<u>U</u>GHTER
<u>R</u>IGHT
KI<u>N</u>G
<u>E</u>VIL
EHU<u>D</u>
J<u>A</u>EL
RELAP<u>S</u>E
DEL<u>I</u>VERED
GI<u>D</u>EON
D<u>E</u>BORAH

SOON THEY TURNED ASIDE

RUTH

The clues from the NRSV translation will lead you to uncover the climax of this story of a faithful, foreign woman—a statement which also contains foreshadowing. Take the boxed letters from each clue to insert in the blanks at the bottom of the page.

1. Elimelech left his home in Judah due to _ ❑ _ _ _. (1:1-2)
2. The birth of and books of ❑ _ _ _ _ _ follow the book of Ruth.
3. Ruth found favor in the sight of _ ❑ _ _. (Ch. 2)
4. The mother-in-law whom Ruth would not abandon was ❑ _ _ _ _. (1:16-18)
5. The family's hometown was _ _ _ ❑ _ _ _ _ _, which means "house of bread". (1:1)
6. Legal property transactions were conducted at the _ ❑ _ _ of a town. (4:1-6)
7. The Old Testament book which precedes Ruth is _ _ _ _ _ ❑.
8. Boaz filled Ruth's cloak with ❑ _ _ _ _ _, so she would not return empty-handed. (3:15)
9. Because she returned home ❑ _ _ _ _, Naomi believed the LORD had dealt bitterly with her. (1:21)
10. The son born to Ruth and Boaz was named _ _ ❑ _; he became grandfather to David. (4:17)
11. People at the gate were _ _ _ ❑ _ _ _ _ _ to the transaction of Boaz's acquisition. (4:11)
12. At mealtime, Boaz offered Ruth ❑ _ _ _ _. (2:14)
13. Boaz commended Ruth for her _ ❑ _ _ _ _ _. (3:10)
14. Naomi sent Ruth to the _ _ ❑ _ _ _ _ _ floor one night after the harvest. (3:3)
15. Ruth's idea to provide food was to _ _ _ _ ❑ the grain following the reapers. (2:2)

❑ ❑❑❑ ❑❑❑

❑❑❑❑ ❑❑❑❑

Answer Key to **RUTH**

F<u>A</u>MINE
<u>S</u>AMUEL
B<u>O</u>AZ
<u>N</u>AOMI
BET<u>H</u>LEHEM
G<u>A</u>TE
JUDGE<u>S</u>
<u>B</u>ARLEY
<u>E</u>MPTY
OB<u>E</u>D
WIT<u>N</u>ESSES
<u>B</u>READ
L<u>O</u>YALTY
TH<u>R</u>ESHING
GLEA<u>N</u>

A SON HAS BEEN BORN

I and II SAMUEL

Discover this message of David's, which is a lament with applications wider than he imagined. Use the indicated letter of each clue word to fill in the squares below. All references are from the NRSV translation, with I = 1st Samuel & II = 2nd Samuel.

1. David sinned with _ _ _ ❏ _ _ _ _ _, wife of Uriah. (II, 11:3)
2. Eli's sons were really _ _ ❏ _ _ _ _ _ _ _! (I, 2:12)
3. Hannah's song of deliverance claims that the LORD has set the ❏ _ _ _ _ on his pillars of the earth. (I, 2:8)
4. The popular slogan claimed Saul had killed his ❏ _ _ _ _ _ _ _ _, and David his ten ____. (I, 18:7; 21:11)
5. In the tradition of other barren women of the Bible, ❏ _ _ _ _ _ prayed to the LORD for a son. (I, 1:2-20)
6. David conquered _ ❏ _ _ _ _ _ _ _ before becoming king of Israel. (II, 5:6)
7. While his head was stuck in an oak tree, _ _ _ _ _ _ ❏ was speared three times in the heart, thus ending his revolt against his father. (II, 18:14)
8. When David confessed his guilt about Uriah, the LORD put away his _ ❏ _. (II, 12:13)
9. When possessing the Ark brought a plague upon the Philistines, they returned it to Israel along with a guilt offering of five ❏ _ _ _ mice. (I, Ch. 6)
10. At Hebron, David became king of _ _ _ _ ❏. (II, 2:1-4)
11. The day Samuel anointed David, the _ _ _ _ _ ❏ of the LORD came mightily upon him. (I, 16:13)
12. David played a _ ❏ _ _ to soothe Saul. (I, 16:23)
13. In those days the _ ❏ _ _ _ _ _ _ _ _ mustered for war against Israel. (I, 4:1)
14. Before he was king, _ ❏ _ _ was sent by his father to find lost donkeys. (I, 9:1-4)
15. Saul's daughter accused _ _ ❏ _ _ of shamelessness when he danced before the Ark unclothed. (II, 6:20-23)
16. Saul spoke with a ghost through the medium at ❏ _ _ _ _ after Samuel's death. (I, 28:5-7)
17. These words of David inspired a famous Lutheran hymn: "The LORD is my rock, my ❏ _ _ _ _ _ _ _, and my deliverer." (II, 22:2)
18. To establish Jerusalem as his capital, David had the ❏ _ _ of God brought there. (II, 6:2)
19. _ ❏ _ was an elderly priest at Shiloh who trained Samuel in ministry. (I, 1:9)
20. The boy _ _ _ _ _ ❏ heard the voice of the LORD during the night. (I, 3:1-11)
21. David's father, Jesse, was from _ _ _ _ _ ❏ _ _ _. (I, 16:1)
22. _ _ _ _ _ ❏ told David a parable about a rich man who stole the only lamb of a poor man. (II, 12:1-6)

❏❏❏ ❏❏❏ ❏❏❏❏❏

❏❏❏❏ ❏❏❏❏❏.

Answer Key to **I and II SAMUEL**

BA**T**HSHEBA
SC**O**UNDRELS
WORLD
THOUSANDS
HANNAH
J**E**RUSALEM
ABSALO**M**
S**I**N
GOLD
JUDA**H**
SPIRI**T**
L**Y**RE
P**H**ILISTINES
S**A**UL
DA**V**ID
ENDOR
FORTRESS
ARK
EL**I**
SAMUE**L**
BETH**L**EHEM
NATHA**N**

HOW THE MIGHTY HAVE FALLEN

I and II KINGS

Throughout the monarchy, there is tension between the divine promise and exclusive worship of the LORD. Follow this history by solving the clues (NRSV translation), then taking the indicated letters of the answers to fill in the blanks that follow. You will uncover a repeated problem the people had. (I = 1st Kings; II = 2nd Kings)

1. At the beginning of these books, David is very _ _ ❑. (I, 1:1; 1:15)
2. If his son will walk in his ways, the LORD will _ _ _ _ _ _ ❑ _ _ his word and the king will prosper. (I, 2:4)
3. The priest who anointed Solomon king was _ _ ❑ _ _. (I, 1:39)
4. The elder son of David, _ _ _ ❑ _ _ _ _, plotted to get the throne from Solomon. (I, 2:13-23)
5. Solomon married a daughter of _ _ _ _ _ ❑ _. (I, 3:1)
6. All Israel stood in awe of Solomon because they perceived the wisdom of God which enabled him to execute _ _ _ ❑ _ _ _. (I, 3:28)
7. The labor to build the Temple was ❑ _ _ _ _ _ _ _ _ _ _, or forced. (I, 5:13)
8. If the people would obey the LORD, the LORD agreed to dwell with Israel and not _❑ _ _ _ _ _ his people. (I, 6:13)
9. If the people forsake the LORD and instead _ ❑ _ _ _ _ _, worship and serve other gods, then the LORD would bring disaster upon them. (I, 9:9)
10. Solomon angered the LORD by building a high ❑ _ _ _ _ for idol worship, influenced by his many foreign wives. (I, 11:7-8)
11. Due to Jeroboam's failure, the LORD will strike _ _ _ _ _ ❑ and scatter the people. (I, 14:15-16)
12. A powerful prophet who performed miracles was ❑ _ _ _ _ _ _. (I, Ch. 17)
13. The word of the LORD in Elijah's mouth is _ _ _ ❑ _. (I, 17:24)
14. _ _ _ ❑ _ _ _ was the queen who arranged the death of Naboth. (I, Ch. 21)
15. Elijah passed his mantle to his successor, _ ❑ _ _ _ _. (II, Ch. 2)
16. Elisha gave instructions for Naaman to be cured of _ _ _ _ _ _ ❑. (II, Ch. 5)
17. The ruthless queen Athaliah destroyed her own ❑ _ _ _ _ _. (II, 11:1-4)
18. Priest Jehoiada renewed the _❑ _ _ _ _ _ _ with the LORD, the king, and the people. (II, 11:17)
19. A dead man whose body was thrown into Elisha's grave, came to ❑ _ _ _ again. (II, 13:21)
20. The LORD saw the distress of _ _ _ _ _ ❑. (II, 14:26)
21. King _ _ _ ❑ _ _ _ _ was able to restore some of the borders of Israel. (II, 14:28)
22. Because Israel ❑ _ _ _ _ _ _ _ _ other gods and did wicked things, the LORD was provoked to anger. (II, 17:7)
23. Assyria besieged Samaria for ❑ _ _ _ _ years. (II, 17:5)
24. Only the tribe _ _ _ _ ❑ was not removed from the LORD's sight. (II, 17:18)
25. As was foretold, Israel was ❑ _ _ _ _ _ to Assyria. (II, 17:23)
26. The LORD told Hezekiah that all would be carried to _ _ _ _ ❑ _ _ and nothing would remain. (II, 20:17)
27. King _ ❑ _ _ _ _ instituted reforms after the book of the law was found during Temple repairs. (II, 22:1-2)
28. Judah and Jerusalem so angered the LORD that he expelled them from his _ ❑ _ _ _ _ _ _. (II, 24:20)
29. Because of his promise to ❑ _ _ _ _, the LORD will always keep Jerusalem his own. (I, 11:36)

- - -   - - -   - - - - - - - - -   - - - - - -   - - -   - - - -

Answer Key to **I and II KINGS**

OL<u>D</u>
ESTABL<u>I</u>SH
ZA<u>D</u>OK
ADO<u>N</u>IJAH
PHARA<u>O</u>H
JUS<u>T</u>ICE
<u>C</u>ONSCRIPTED
F<u>O</u>RSAKE
E<u>M</u>BRACE
<u>P</u>LACE
ISRAE<u>L</u>
<u>E</u>LIJAH
TRU<u>T</u>H
JE<u>Z</u>EBEL
E<u>L</u>ISHA
LEPROS<u>Y</u>
<u>F</u>AMILY
C<u>O</u>VENANT
<u>L</u>IFE
ISRAE<u>L</u>
JER<u>O</u>BOAM
<u>W</u>ORSHIPED
<u>T</u>HREE
JUDA<u>H</u>
<u>E</u>XILED
BABY<u>L</u>ON
J<u>O</u>SIAH
P<u>R</u>ESENCE
<u>D</u>AVID

DID NOT COMPLETELY FOLLOW THE LORD

ESTHER

The hidden message for this puzzle describes the experience of Esther's people. Using the clues from the NRSV translation, fill in the blanks. Then take the boxed letter from each answer to find the message of the blank spaces at the bottom of the page.

1. Esther won the king's devotion and ☐ _ _ _ _. (2:17)
2. The _ _ ☐ were lots cast to determine the time for the destruction of the Jews. (3:7)
3. Mordecai charged Esther not to reveal her _ _ ☐ _ _ _ or kindred. (2:20)
4. The Agagite _ _ ☐ _ _, as grand vizier, was to receive obeisance from all under the king. (3:1-3)
5. The Persian queen _ _ ☐ _ _ _ was banished, thereby getting her wish not to be seen by the king. (1:11-12)
6. Cousin _ ☐ _ _ _ _ _ brought up the orphaned Esther. (2:7)
7. Esther concludes with letters sent to all Jewish people and their descendants to observe the days of _ _ ☐ _ _ forever. (Ch. 9)
8. Three times the text emphasizes that despite slaughtering 75,810 people, the Jews laid no hand on the _ _ _ _ _ _ ☐. (9:10,15,16)
9. With no mention of prayer, miracles, the covenant, or even _ ☐ _, this book's inclusion in the canon was disputed. Martin Luther wished the book had never been written!
10. In a dramatic turn of events, Haman had to lead Mordecai, regally robed, through the open square on a royal horse which wore a _ _ _ ☐ _. (6:8)
11. Mordecai told Esther that if she kept _ ☐ _ _ _ _ _, deliverance would come from elsewhere, but she would perish. (4:14)
12. These fellows who guarded the harem were _ _ ☐ _ _ _ _. (2:14-15)
13. The events of this story took place in the ☐ _ _ _ _ year of the reign of Ahasueras. (1:3)
14. The book which follows Esther in the Old Testament is _ ☐ _.
15. Justice for Haman meant using the ☐ _ _ _ _ _ _. (7:10)
16. Mordecai suggested that Esther had come to _ _ _ _ ☐ dignity for such a time. (4:14)
17. The ruler of the Persian empire was _ _ ☐ _ _ _ _ _ _. (1:1)
18. On the _ _ _ ☐ day, Esther approached the king without permission. (5:1)
19. It was during a second _ _ ☐ _ _ _ _ that Esther exposed the plight of her people.(5:8; 6:14)
20. Zeresh prophesied to her husband, Haman, that he will not prevail if Mordecai is of the _ ☐ _ _ _ _ people. (6:13)
21. Recruits to the harem underwent a six-month _ _ ☐ _ _ _ _ _ treatment. (2:3,9,12)
22. The setting for the story is the Persian city of _ _ ☐ _. (1:2)

☐ ☐ ☐ ☐   ☐ ☐ ☐ ☐ ☐ ☐   ☐ ☐ ☐ ☐
☐ ☐ ☐ ☐ ☐ ☐ ☐ ☐

Answer Key to **ESTHER**

F̲AVOR
PUR̲
PE̲OPLE
HA̲MAN
VAS̲HTI
MO̲RDECAI
PUR̲IM
PLUNDER̲
GO̲D
CROW̲N
SI̲LENCE
EUN̲UCHS
T̲HIRD
JO̲B
G̲ALLOWS
ROYAL
AHA̲SUERAS
THIRD̲
BAN̲QUET
JE̲WISH
COS̲METIC
S̲USA

FROM SORROW INTO GLADNESS

JOB

Find Job's confession by first filling in the missing words in each clue, using the NRSV references. Then take the letters in the boxes to fill in the spaces at the bottom.

1. The abode of the dead is called the _ ▢ _, also known as Sheol. (33:24)
2. God challenges Job to recognize who is the creator: "Surely you ▢ _ _ _." (38:5)
3. "Where were you when I laid the _ _ _ ▢ _ _ _ _ _ _ of the earth?" asked the LORD. (38:4)
4. Job, a blameless and upright man, feared _ ▢ _ and turned away from evil. (1:1)
5. According to Bildad, "Our days on earth are but a _ _ _ _ _ ▢." (8:9)
6. The LORD _ _ _ ▢ _ _ _ _ the fortunes of Job and blessed his latter days. (42:10)
7. The LORD answered Job out of a _ ▢ _ _ _ _ _ _ _. (38:1)
8. Job's visitor, the Naamathite was named _ _ _ _ ▢ _. (2:11)
9. Before his suffering, Job was honored at the city _ _ ▢ _ by all. (29:7)
10. One of Job's responses claimed, "A ▢ _ _ _ _ _, born of woman, few of days and full of trouble." (14:1)
11. The LORD accepted Job's _ _ _ ▢ _ _. (42:9)
12. According to Eliphaz, "Human beings are _ _ ▢ _ to trouble just as sparks fly upward." (5:7)
13. In Job's response to his friends, he said, "I will not _ _ ▢ to your face." (6:28)
14. God sees all in judgment and the wicked are _ _ _ _ _ _ ▢, according to Elihu. (34:25)
15. Job's visitor, the Temanite, was named ▢ _ _ _ _ _ _. (2:11)
16. Job's fourth visitor, the son of Barachel the Buzite, was ▢ _ _ _ _. (32:2)
17. The Old Testament book which follows the book of Job is _ _ _ _ ▢ _.
18. Job stated, "For I know that my _ _ _ ▢ _ _ _ _ lives." (19:25)
19. Job did not put his _ ▢ _ _ _ in gold. (31:24)
20. Job's visitor, the Shuhite, was named _ _ ▢ _ _ _ (2:11)
21. Job said to the LORD, "If I _ ▢ _, you watch me." (10:14)
22. When Job's friends arrived and saw his suffering, they sat with him _ _ ▢ _ _ days and _ _ _ _ nights without saying one word. (2:13)
23. Job lamented, "_ _ _ ▢ _ I came from my mother's womb, and _ _ _ _ shall I return there; the LORD gave, and the LORD has taken away." (1:21)
24. Job's wife told him, "_ _ _ ▢ _ God, and die." (2:9)

▢ ▢▢▢▢ ▢▢▢▢ ▢▢

▢▢▢▢▢▢▢ ▢▢▢▢▢.

Answer Key to **JOB**

P<u>I</u>T
<u>K</u>NOW
FOU<u>N</u>DATION
G<u>O</u>D
SHADO<u>W</u>
RES<u>T</u>ORED
W<u>H</u>IRLWIND
ZOPH<u>A</u>R
GA<u>TE</u>
<u>M</u>ORTAL
PRA<u>Y</u>ER
BO<u>R</u>N
LI<u>E</u>
CRUSHE<u>D</u>
<u>E</u>LIPHAZ
<u>E</u>LIHU
PSAL<u>MS</u>
RED<u>E</u>EMER
T<u>R</u>UST
BI<u>L</u>DAD
S<u>I</u>N
SE<u>V</u>EN
NAK<u>E</u>D
CUR<u>SE</u>

I KNOW THAT MY REDEEMER LIVES

PSALMS

1. The Psalms were first written in the language of ❑ _ _ _ _ _ .
2. O sing to the LORD a new song, for he has done marvelous _ _ ❑ _ _ _ . (Ps. 98:1)
3. But you, O LORD, are a God merciful and gracious, ❑ _ _ _ to anger and abounding in steadfast love and faithfulness. (Ps. 86:15)
4. How could we sing the LORD's ❑ _ _ _ in a foreign land? (Ps. 137:4)
5. I call upon the LORD, who is _ _ _ ❑ _ _ to be praised, so I shall be saved from my enemies. (Ps. 18:3)
6. As a _ ❑ _ _ longs for flowing streams, so my soul longs for you, O God. (Ps. 42:1)
7. The _ _ ❑ _ of the LORD is the beginning of wisdom. (Ps. 111:10)
8. Out of the ❑ _ _ _ _ _ I cry to you, O LORD, Lord, hear my voice! (Ps. 130:1)
9. I will _ _ _ ❑ _ _ _ my transgressions to the LORD, and you forgave the guilt of my sin. (Ps. 32:5)
10. O LORD, you have _ _ ❑ _ _ _ _ _ me and known me. (Ps. 139:1)
1. I was glad when they ❑ _ _ _ to me, 'Let us go to the house of the LORD'. (Ps. 122:1)
12. Be _ ❑ _ _ _ and know that I am God. (Ps. 46:10)
13. The heavens are telling the _ ❑ _ _ _ of God; and the firmament proclaims his handiwork. (Ps. 19:1)
14. For a day in your _ ❑ _ _ _ is better than a thousand elsewhere. (Ps. 84:10)
15. By the _ _ ❑ _ _ _ of Babylon—there we sat down and there we wept when we remembered Zion. (Ps. 137:1)
16. What shall I _ ❑ _ _ _ _ to the LORD for all his bounty to me? (Ps. 116:12)
17. For a thousand _ ❑ _ _ _ in your sight are like yesterday when it is past. (Ps. 90:4)
18. Make a joyful ❑ _ _ _ _ to the LORD, all the earth; Worship the LORD with gladness; come into his presence with singing. (Ps. 100:1)
19. The king credited with the composition of many psalms is ❑ _ _ _ _ .
20. Surely goodness and mercy shall follow me all the days of my life, and I shall dwell in the _ _ ❑ _ _ of the LORD my whole life long. (Ps. 23:6)
21. Make me to know _ _ _ ❑ ways, O LORD; teach me your paths. (Ps. 25:4)
22. The LORD will keep your going out and your coming in from this _ _ _ ❑ on and forevermore. (Ps. 121:8)
23. I will lift up the cup of ❑ _ _ _ _ _ _ _ _ and call on the name of the LORD. (Ps. 116:13)
24. The LORD is my rock, my ❑ _ _ _ _ _ _ _ , and my deliverer, my God, my rock in whom I take refuge, my shield, and the horn of my salvation, my stronghold. (Ps. 18:2— *This, by the way, is the longest string of divine epithets in the Bible!*)
25. The book which comes before Psalms in our Bibles is _ ❑ _ .
26. I wait for the LORD, my soul waits, and in his _ _ ❑ _ I hope. (Ps. 130:5)
27. _ _ _ ❑ _ _ the LORD builds the house, those who built it labor in vain. (Ps. 127:1)
28. The book which comes after Psalms in our Bibles is _ _ _ ❑ _ _ _ _ .
29. A frequently occurring, yet unknown, Hebrew word which may be a liturgical instruction is _ ❑ _ _ _ . (Psalm 3)
30. Let everything that breathes _ ❑ _ _ _ _ the LORD! Praise the LORD! (Ps. 150:6)

Hidden message: _ _ _ _ _ _ _ _ _ _ _ _ _ _ _ _ _ _ _ _ _ _ _ _ _ _ _ _ _ _ .

Answer Key to **PSALMS**

H̲EBREW
THI̲NGS
S̲LOW
S̲ONG
WORT̲HY
DE̲ER
FEA̲R
D̲EPTHS
CONF̲ESS
SEA̲RCHED
S̲AID
ST̲ILL
GL̲ORY
CO̲URTS
RIV̲ERS
RET̲URN
YE̲ARS
N̲OISE
D̲AVID
HOU̲SE
YOUR̲
TIME
S̲ALVATION
F̲ORTRESS
JO̲B
WOR̲D
UNLE̲SS
PROV̲ERBS
SEL̲AH
PR̲AISE

HIS STEADFAST LOVE ENDURES FOREVER

128

ECCLESIASTES

From the writings of wisdom attributed to Qoheleth, the Preacher, we get many observations of life, but the recurring theme suggests we only chase after wind! Find the missing words from these quotations (NRSV translation) for the spaces at the bottom, to reveal the repeating theme of Qoheleth.

1. Never be _ ❑ _ _ with your mouth. (5:2)
2. The Preacher claims to be a "king over _ _ _ _ _ ❑ in Jerusalem". (1:12)
3. A living dog is better than a dead ❑ _ _ _. (9:4)
4. For _ _ _ _ _ _ _ ❑ _ _ there is a season. (3:1)
5. ❑ _ _ _ _ is the sleep of laborers. (5:12)
6. So I commend enjoyment for there is nothing better for people under the sun than to eat, and drink, and enjoy _ _ _ _ _ _ _ ❑ _ _. (8:15)
7. The race is not to the swift, nor the battle to the strong, but time and _ _ ❑ _ _ _ happen to them all. (9:11)
8. The _ ❑ _ of the matter; all has been heard. (12:13)
9. There is _ _ _ _ ❑ _ _ new under the sun. (1:9)
10. ❑ _ _ are better than one. (4:9)
11. Remember your creator in the days of your ❑ _ _ _ _, before the days of trouble come. (12:1)

❑ ❑ ❑

❑ ❑

❑ ❑ ❑ ❑ ❑ .

Answer Key to **ECCLESIASTES**

R<u>A</u>SH
ISRAE<u>L</u>
<u>L</u>ION
EVERYTH<u>I</u>NG
<u>S</u>WEET
THEMSEL<u>V</u>ES
CH<u>A</u>NCE
E<u>N</u>D
NOTH<u>I</u>NG
<u>T</u>WO
<u>Y</u>OUTH

ALL IS VANITY

Use the boxed letters from the clue words to fill in the squares reading across to discover one of the LORD's messages to Isaiah.   (All clues are from the NRSV translation.)

1. The introduction to Isaiah states the text came to the prophet in a _ _ _ ❑ _ _ (1:1)
2. As he saw the heavenly court, a seraph touched a live _ _ ❑ to his mouth. (6:6-7)
3. After the LORD's wrath is poured out on Judah and Jerusalem, there will be a renewal of the holy on ❑ _ _ _ _ _ _ _ _ .(4:2-5)
4. The LORD's judgment will occur since his children are a sinful _ _ ❑ _ _ . (1:4)
5. After the judgment of the LORD, peace will be universal: "They shall beat their swords into _ _ _ _ _ ❑ _ _ _ and their spears into pruning hooks." (2:4)
6. Under a future ruler (a Messiah), peace will extend to all creation: "The wolf shall live with the lamb, the _ ❑ _ _ _ _ shall lie down with the kid., the calf and the lion and the fatling together, and a little child shall lead them." (11:6)
7. The LORD hates ritual purification that lacks a penitent heart: "Trample my courts no more; bringing offerings is ❑ _ _ _ _ _ ; incense is an abomination." (1:13)
8. Isaiah said God is behind all historical events, even the actions of foreign nations: "I will punish the world for its evil, and the _ ❑ _ _ _ for their iniquity." (13:11)
9. The first _ ❑ _ _ _ _ against foreign nations is addressed to Babylon. (13:1)
10. The LORD expected his vineyard to yield _ _ _ _ _ ❑ . (5:1-4)
11. With the Lord on his throne; the hem of God's robe filled the ❑ _ _ _ _ _ .(6:1)
12. The LORD will cause the invasion by ❑ _ _ _ _ _ _ . (8:4-8)
13. When the new heir to the throne is born, a new age will begin: "The people who walked in _ _ _ _ ❑ _ _ _ have seen a great light. (9:2)
14. "For a _ _ _ _ ❑ has been born for us, a son given to us; authority rests upon his shoulders; and he is named Wonderful Counselor, Mighty God, Everlasting Father, Prince of Peace." (9:6)
15. Isaiah was to walk barefoot and naked for three years as a _ ❑ _ _ for how the exiles would be shamed. (20:2-4)
16. Destruction was decreed for the people, but a _ _ _ _ ❑ _ _ would return. (10:22)
17. After the exile, God would renew the covenant to his people: _ _ ❑ _ _ _ _ , O _ _ _ my people, says your God. (40:1)
18. As the people will be returned, so will the glory of the LORD: "A voice cries out 'In the wilderness prepare the way of the LORD, make _ ❑ _ _ _ _ _ _ in the desert a highway for our God.'" (40:3)
19. God will be compassionate: "He will feed his flock like a _ _ _ _ ❑ _ _ _ .(40:11)
20. In chapters 40-48, Israel is called the LORD's _ ❑ _ _ _ _ _ (42:1)
21. The Lord GOD's house shall be called a house of prayer for _ ❑ _ peoples. (56:7)
22. The call to repentance offers to all nations a heavenly banquet: "I will make with you an everlasting _ _ _ _ _ ❑ _ _ ." (55:3)
23. "From new moon to new moon, and from ❑ _ _ _ _ _ _ to _ _ _ , all flesh shall come to worship before me, says the LORD." (66:23)
24. The LORD says, "For I am about to _ _ _ ❑ _ new heavens and a new earth; the former things shall not be remembered or come to mind." (65:17)

— .

Answer Key to **ISAIAH**

V<u>I</u>SION
CO<u>A</u>L
<u>M</u>OUNT ZION
NA<u>T</u>ION
PLOWS<u>H</u>ARES
L<u>E</u>OPARD
<u>F</u>UTILE
W<u>I</u>CKED
O<u>R</u>ACLE
GRAPE<u>S</u>
<u>T</u>EMPLE
<u>A</u>SSYRIA
DARK<u>N</u>ESS
CHIL<u>D</u>
S<u>I</u>GN
REMN<u>A</u>NT
CO<u>M</u>FORT
STRAIG<u>H</u>T
SHEP<u>H</u>ERD
S<u>E</u>RVANT
AL<u>L</u>
COVEN<u>A</u>NT
<u>S</u>ABBATH
CREA<u>T</u>E

I AM THE FIRST AND I AM THE LAST

EZEKIEL

Use the clues (from the NRSV translation) to fill in the missing words, then take the boxed letters to place in the spaces below to find Ezekiel's message (which is mentioned over fifteen times in the book.)

1. God's term of address to Ezekiel is _ _ _ ❑ _ _. (2:1; 3:1; 4:1; 5:1)
2. Four-sided, winged creatures with wheels are _ ❑ _ _ _ _ _ _. (Ch. 1 & 10)
3. From the new temple will flow a sacred _ _ _ ❑ _. (Ch. 47)
4. Ezekiel had a vision of a _ _ _ _ _ ❑ full of dry bones (37:1-6)
5. The LORD gave a ❑ _ _ _ _ _ to Ezekiel to eat. (3:1)
6. GOD has no pleasure in the _ _ _ _ ❑ of anyone. (18:32)
7. Ezekiel had to carry _ _ _ _ ❑ _ _ through a hole in the wall (12:3-7)
8. Ezekiel was among the _ _ _ ❑ _ _ in the land of the Chaldeans. (1:1)
9. God's adjective for the house of Judah is _ _ _ _ ❑ _ _ _ _ _. (2:5-7)
10. "You shall ❑ _ _ _ that I am the LORD." (20:42)
11. The book _ _ ❑ _ _ _ follows Ezekiel in the Old Testament.
12. The visions showed the _ _ ❑ _ _ of the LORD (1:28; 3:23)
13. GOD told Ezekiel to shave his head with a _ ❑ _ _ _. (5:1)
14. The book _ _ _ _ _ ❑ _ _ _ _ _ _ precedes Ezekiel in the Old Testament
15. In renewing his covenant, God desired to remove the exiles' ❑ _ _ _ _ of stone and give them a _ _ _ _ of flesh. (11:19-20; 36:26)
16. God promised to remember and establish the _ _ _ _ _ ❑ _ _. (16:60; 37:26)
17. God told the story of leading Israel out of _ _ _ _ ❑. (Ch.20)
18. Ezekiel's father was named _ _ _ ❑. (1:3)
19. In his oracles against the nations, Ezekiel was told to set his _ ❑ _ _ either toward or against these nations. (Ch. 25-28)
20. When his wife died, the LORD told him not to ❑ _ _ _ _. (24:16)
21. Ezekiel had a vision of the new ❑ _ _ _ _ _ _.(Ch. 40)
22. GOD will search for his _ ❑ _ _ _ and care for the flock (Ch. 34)
23. The hand of the LORD _ ❑ _ _ _ _ _ _ all the spaces and distances of the new temple. (Ch 40-42)
24. There are two fables about _ _ _ ❑ _ _ in chapter 17.
25. The LORD wanted the house of Israel to repent and turn away from _ _ ❑ _ _. (Ch. 14)
26. God gave instructions for various types of _ _ _ _ ❑ _ _ _ _. (45:10-17)
27. The name of the new city for the tribe of Israel will be: "The _ _ _ ❑ Is There". (48:35)

❑❑❑❑ ❑❑❑❑❑ ❑❑❑❑

❑❑❑❑ ❑ ❑❑

❑❑❑ ❑❑❑❑.

Answer Key to **EZEKIEL**

MOR<u>T</u>AL
C<u>H</u>ERUBIM
RIV<u>E</u>R
VALLE<u>Y</u>
<u>S</u>CROLL
DEAT<u>H</u>
BAGG<u>A</u>GE
EXI<u>L</u>ES
REBEL<u>L</u>IOUS
<u>K</u>NOW
DA<u>N</u>IEL
GL<u>O</u>RY
S<u>W</u>ORD
LAMEN<u>T</u>ATIONS
<u>H</u>EART
COVEN<u>A</u>NT
EGYP<u>T</u>
BUZ<u>I</u>
F<u>A</u>CE
<u>M</u>OURN
<u>T</u>EMPLE
S<u>H</u>EEP
M<u>E</u>ASURED
EAG<u>L</u>ES
ID<u>O</u>LS
OFFE<u>R</u>INGS
LOR<u>D</u>

THEY SHALL KNOW THAT I AM THE LORD

DANIEL

To learn of something exciting from the book of Daniel, use the clues (references from the NRSV translation) to find the missing words across, then place the boxed letter into the spaces below.

1. Daniel gave the Babylonian king a trustworthy _ _ _ _ _ _ _ ❑ _ _ _ _ _ of his dream of a statue. (2:16)
2. In the fiery furnace with Meshach, Shadrach, and Abednego was seen a _ _ _ _ _ ❑ man with "the appearance of a god". (3:25)
3. For refusing to worship a king's golden statue, the Israelite youths were thrown into a _ _ _ _ _ _ ❑. (3:1-23)
4. The Babylonian palace master gave Daniel the name _ _ _ _ _ ❑ _ _ _ _ _. (1:7)
5. The vision of the end of time is explained to Daniel by _ ❑ _ _ _ _ _. (8:15-17)
6. An Israelite youth named _ _ ❑ _ _ _ is designated to be educated in the Babylonian king's court, fed royally, and taught Chaldean literature. (1:4-6)
7. When Daniel survived the lions' den, King Darius was exceedingly glad and decreed all people should tremble and fear _ _ ❑. (6:26)
8. In Daniel's vision, an Ancient One took a throne of fiery flames with ❑ _ _ _ _ _ of burning fire. (7:9-10)
9. For interpreting the mysterious writing, Daniel was given a _ _ ❑ _ _ _ cloak, a chain of gold, and a high rank. (5:29)
10. The great protector of all people who will arise at the end of time is _ ❑ _ _ _ _ _. (12:1)
11. In Daniel's second dream interpretation, the king is symbolized as a ❑ _ _ _. (4:10-26)
12. King Belshazzar saw a _ ❑ _ _ _ _ making a message on the wall. (5:5)
13. For praying, in defiance of King Darius' edict, Daniel was thrown into a _ _ ❑ of lions. (6:9-16)
14. Daniel's preferred food was _ _ ❑ _ _ _ _ _ _ _. (1:12,16)
15. The message on the wall predicted that the kingdom would be _ _ _ ❑ _ _ _. (5:28)
16. Nebuchadnezzar decreed no one should utter _ _ _ ❑ _ _ _ _ _ against their God. (3:29)
17. The Old Testament book which follows the book of Daniel is _ ❑ _ _ _.
18. The woman who recognized Daniel's worth was the _ _ _ _ ❑. (5:10)
19. After his sentence of living like an animal, the King _ _ _ ❑ _ _ his eyes to heaven in blessing. (4:33-34)
20. _ _ _ _ _ ❑ _ _ _ _ _ _ _ was the Babylonian king who besieged Jerusalem. (1:1)
21. Daniel was told to keep the words _ ❑ _ _ _ _ and the book sealed till the time of the end. (12:4,9)
22. Everyone found ❑ _ _ _ _ _ _ in the book shall be delivered. (12:1)
23. Daniel had insight into visions and _ _ _ ❑ _ _. (1:17)
24. The Old Testament book which precedes the book of Daniel is _ _ _ _ _ _ ❑.
25. Many who sleep shall awake to everlasting ❑ _ _ _. (12:2)

❑❑❑ ❑❑❑❑❑❑❑❑❑❑❑

❑❑ ❑❑ ❑❑❑ ❑❑❑❑.

135

Answer Key to **DANIEL**

INTERPRE<u>T</u>ATION
FOURT<u>H</u>
FURNAC<u>E</u>
BELTES<u>H</u>AZZAR
G<u>A</u>BRIEL
DA<u>N</u>IEL
GO<u>D</u>
<u>W</u>HEELS
PU<u>R</u>PLE
M<u>I</u>CHAEL
<u>T</u>REE
F<u>I</u>NGER
DE<u>N</u>
VE<u>G</u>ETABLES
D<u>I</u>VIDED
BLA<u>S</u>PHEMY
H<u>O</u>SEA
QUEE<u>N</u>
LIF<u>T</u>ED
NEBUC<u>H</u>ADNEZZAR
SECR<u>E</u>T
<u>W</u>RITTEN
DRE<u>A</u>MS
EZEKIE<u>L</u>
<u>L</u>IFE

THE HANDWRITING IS ON THE WALL

HOSEA

Fill in the missing words (NRSV translation), then use the boxed letters to spell out Hosea's message in the boxes reading across the bottom of the page. The book of Hosea tells of the LORD's indictment of the people, a situation echoed in Hosea's own marriage.

1. In referring to the time of Israel's deliverance from the land of Egypt, she was at that time in the days of her _ _ _ ❑ _. (2:15)
2. When the people seek the LORD, they will not find him, for he has _ _ _ ❑ _ _ _ _ _ from them. (5:6)
3. The name of Hosea's unfaithful wife was _ _ _ ❑ _. (1:3)
4. In Hosea's speeches, the Northern Kingdom (Israel) is often called by the name of its largest tribe, _ _ _ ❑ _ _ _. (5:3)
5. The word of the LORD came to Hosea during the reign of King _ ❑ _ _ _ _ _ of Israel. (1:1)
6. Hosea accused the priests of being greedy for the _ _ ❑ _ _ _ _ of the people. (4:8)
7. The LORD will exile the people to the land of _ _ ❑ _ _ _ _. (9:3; 10:6)
8. The book which precedes Hosea in the Bible is _ _ ❑ _ _ _.
9. The book which follows Hosea in the Bible is _ ❑ _ _.
10. Because they have ❑ _ _ _ _ _ _ _ _ the law of God, he will forget their children. (4:6)
11. The name of the "idol" the people worshipped was _ _ ❑ _. (2:13, 17)
12. God reminded the people that he had been their LORD since he led them from Egypt, and it was he who fed them in the _ ❑ _ _ _ _ _ _ _. (13:5)
13. When Israel was young, God loved him and called him out of _ _ _ _ ❑. (11:1)
14. Hosea's plea to return to the LORD claims "on the _ ❑ _ _ _ day he will raise us up, that we may live before him." (6:2)
15. The LORD's metaphor claims, "I will take you for my _ _ ❑ _ forever; I will take you for my ____ in righteousness and in justice, in steadfast love, and in mercy. I will take you for my ____ in faithfulness; and you shall know the LORD. (2:19-20)
16. Because of Israel's idolatry, the LORD will _ ❑ _ _ _ _ her. (2:13)
17. Images of a _ _ ❑ _, made in Samaria, are rejected and anger the LORD. (8:5)
18. After the punishment, Israel will be restored as a luxuriant _ _ ❑ _. (10:1)
19. Because Ephraim has been silly and without sense, it is compared to a _ _ _ ❑. (7:11)
20. The capital of the Northern Kingdom was ❑ _ _ _ _ _ _. (13:16)
21. The LORD will heal the people's _ _ ❑ _ _ _ _ _ _ _ and love them freely. (14:4)

❑ ❑ ❑ ❑ ❑   ❑ ❑   ❑ ❑

❑ ❑ ❑ ❑ ❑ ❑ ❑ ❑ ❑ ❑ ❑

Answer Key to **HOSEA**

YOU<u>T</u>H
WIT<u>H</u>DRAWN
GOM<u>E</u>R
EPH<u>R</u>AIM
J<u>E</u>ROBOAM
IN<u>I</u>QUITY
AS<u>S</u>YRIA
DA<u>N</u>IEL
J<u>O</u>EL
<u>F</u>ORGOTTEN
BA<u>A</u>L
W<u>I</u>LDERNESS
EGYP<u>T</u>
<u>T</u>HIRD
WI<u>F</u>E
P<u>U</u>NISH
CA<u>L</u>F
VI<u>N</u>E
DOV<u>E</u>
<u>S</u>AMARIA
DI<u>S</u>LOYALTY

THERE IS NO FAITHFULNESS

AMOS

Central to the message of Amos is the sentiment expressed at the bottom of this page, which you will uncover by finding the missing words in each clue (NRSV), then taking the boxed letters to fill in the blank boxes below.

1. Amos' oracles repeatedly say the LORD will not revoke punishment for the many _ _ _ _ ☐ _ _ _ _ _ _ _ _ _ of the nations. (1:3,6,9,11,13)
2. Let _ _ _ _ _ _ ☐ roll down like waters. (5:24)
3. Amos' fourth vision was a basket of _ _ _ _ ☐ _ fruit. (8:1)
4. The start of Amos' prophecies coincided with an _ _ _ _ _ _ _ _ ☐ _ . (1:1)
5. In Amos' fifth vision, the LORD was standing beside an _ _ ☐ _ _ . (9:1)
6. Amos' second vision of judgment was a _ ☐ _ _ _ _ of fire. (7:4)
7. Amos' third vision of judgment included a plumb _ _ _ ☐. (7:8)
8. Amos' first vision of judgment was of ☐ _ _ _ _ _ _ . (7:1)
9. The LORD's creation included the constellation _ _ _ ☐ _ (named in Greek for a hunter). (5:8)
10. Amos was a herdsman and a dresser of _ _ _ _ _ _ ☐ _ trees. (7:14)
11. A musician mentioned in 6:5 was _ _ _ _ ☐.
12. Amos' hometown was _ _ _ _ ☐. (1:1)
13. Amos prophesies God's _ _ ☐ _ _ _ _ _ _ _ of the morally corrupt. (1:6)
14. The LORD's creation included the constellation _ _ _ _ _ ☐ _ _ (named in Greek for seven sisters.) (5:8)
15. Seek good and not _ _ _ ☐ that you may live. (5:14)
16. When the fortunes of Israel are restored by the LORD, the mountains and hills will flow with sweet _ ☐ _ _. (9:13)
17. The number of minor prophets in the Old Testament is _ _ _ _ _ ☐ _ .
18. One of God's complaints was directed against those who _ _ _ _ ☐ _ _ the poor. (4:1)

☐☐☐☐ ☐☐☐
☐☐☐☐
☐☐☐ ☐☐☐☐

Answer Key to **AMOS**

TRAN<u>S</u>GRESSIONS
JUSTIC<u>E</u>
SUMM<u>E</u>R
EARTHQUA<u>K</u>E
AL<u>T</u>AR
S<u>H</u>OWER
LIN<u>E</u>
<u>L</u>OCUSTS
ORI<u>O</u>N
SYCAMO<u>R</u>E
DAV<u>I</u>D
TEKO<u>A</u>
PUNISHME<u>N</u>T
PLEIA<u>D</u>ES
EV<u>I</u>L
W<u>I</u>NE
TWEL<u>VE</u>
OPPR<u>E</u>SS

SEEK THE LORD AND LIVE

140

JONAH

To find God's question for Jonah, solve the clues, then use the indicated letter from each response to fill in the empty squares in order.

1. The book which follows Jonah in the Old Testament is _ ☐ _ _ _.
2. The mariners used _ _ _ ☐ to determine Jonah was the cause of the calamity. (1:7)
3. The LORD provided a _ ☐ _ _ to swallow Jonah. (1:17)
4. Jonah was in the belly of the big fish for ☐ _ _ _ _ days and nights ("sign of Jonah"). (1:17)
5. Jonah explained he was displeased because he knew the LORD would ☐ _ _ _ _ _ _. (4:2)
6. One of the LORD's favorite weapons is the _ ☐ _ _. (1:4)
7. The sailors prayed to not be ☐ _ _ _ _ _ of innocent blood. (1:14)
8. A minor prophet, whose name means "Dove", but who is never called a "prophet" in this book is _ _ _ _ ☐.
9. Jonah's proclamation to Nineveh stated it would be _ _ _ _ ☐ _ _ _ _ _. (3:4)
10. The creature which vomited Jonah was a ☐ _ _ _. (2:10)
11. When the sailors were saved from perishing in the raging sea, they feared the LORD and made _ ☐ _ _. (1:16)
12. In his distress, Jonah _ ☐ _ _ _ _. (2:1)
13. Jonah predicted _ _ _ _ ☐ days before Nineveh's fate would occur. (3:4)
14. Deliverance belongs to the _ ☐ _ _. (2:9)
15. The king's proclamation was for all to _ ☐ _ _ from evil and violence. (3:8)
16. The father of Jonah was _ _ _ _ ☐ _ _ (1:1)
17. The book preceding Jonah in the Old Testament is ☐ _ _ _ _ _ _.
18. God appointed a ☐ _ _ _ to teach Jonah a lesson about pity for the ignorant. (4:6)
19. _ _ _ _ _ ☐ _ _ _ _ _ belongs to the LORD. (2:9)
20. The King of Nineveh declared all humans and *animals* should be covered in _ ☐ _ _ _ _ _ _. (3:8)
21. The great and wicked city built by Noah's great grandson was _ _ ☐ _ _ _ _ (1:2)
22. ☐ _ _ changed his mind, and calamity was avoided. (3:10)
23. It would take _ _ ☐ _ _ days to walk across Nineveh. (3:3)
24. When God changed his mind, Jonah became _ _ _ _ ☐. (4:1)

☐☐ ☐☐ ☐☐☐☐☐ ☐☐☐

☐☐☐ ☐☐ ☐☐ ☐☐☐☐☐

Answer Key to **JONAH**

M̲ICAH
LOT̲S
F̲ISH
T̲HREE
R̲ELENT
WI̲ND
G̲UILTY
JONA̲H
OVER̲THROWN
F̲ISH
VO̲WS
PR̲AYED
FORT̲Y
LO̲RD
TU̲RN
AMIT̲TAI
O̲BADIAH
B̲USH
DELIV̲ERANCE
S̲ACKCLOTH
NI̲NEVEH
G̲OD
THR̲EE
ANGR̲Y

IS IT RIGHT FOR YOU TO BE ANGRY

Complete the sentences with the missing words (using NRSV translation clues), then take the boxed letter from each word to spell out the message at the bottom of the page. Then, you will read a recurring message from the LORD.

1. In Zechariah's first vision, he saw four horsemen who _ _ _ ❑ _ _ _ _ _ the earth. (1:10)
2. The LORD commissioned Zechariah to be a _ _ ❑ _ _ _ _ _ of the flock, knowing they were doomed. (11:4+)
3. Zechariah's final vision was of four colored _ _ _ _ _ _ ❑ _ emerging from between two mountains of bronze. (6:1-8)
4. Zechariah saw a surveyor measuring _ _ _ ❑ _ _ _ _ _ in his third night vision. (2:1-5)
5. The second half of this book is divided into units which begin with the title, "An _ ❑ _ _ _ _ ." (9:1; 12:1)
6. After the final battle, the LORD will be _ _ ❑ _ over all the earth. (14:9)
7. The final three chapters of Zechariah describe the coming Day of the LORD with the recurring phrase, "On ❑ _ _ _ day."
8. The new king will be riding a _ ❑ _ _ _ _ rather than a war-horse, because he will be a king of peace. (9:9)
9. With Haggai, which precedes this book, and ❑ _ _ _ _ _ _ , which follows it, there are unifying phrases and themes.
10. 10. The LORD refers to the people of Zion as the _ _ _ _ ❑ of his eye. (2:8)

❑ ❑ ❑ ❑ ❑ ❑   ❑ ❑   ❑ ❑

Answer Key to **ZECHARIAH**

PAT<u>R</u>OLLED
SH<u>E</u>PHERD
CHARIO<u>T</u>S
JER<u>U</u>SALEM
O<u>R</u>ACLE
KI<u>N</u>G
TH<u>A</u>T
D<u>O</u>NKEY
<u>M</u>ALACHI
APPL<u>E</u>

RETURN TO ME

MATTHEW

Fill in the missing words for each clue (NRSV translation), then take the boxed letters to spell out, in the spaces at the bottom of this page, the message of Matthew (as well as Jesus' own message in this Gospel).

1. Only Matthew's Gospel opens with a ❑ _ _ _ _ _ _ _ to show Jesus' ancestry as a son of David and a son of Abraham.

2. A righteous person visited three times by an angel is _ ❑ _ _ _. (2:13)

3. When Jesus had been baptized, a voice from heaven said, "This is my Son, the _ _ _ ❑ _ _ _, with whom I am well pleased." (3:17)

4. "_ _ _ _ _ _ ❑ are those who are persecuted for righteousness' sake, for theirs is the kingdom of heaven." (5:10)

5. The "_ _ ❑ of Man came not to be served but to serve, and to give his life as a ransom for many." (20:28)

6. The first to answer Jesus' call to follow were Simon _ ❑ _ _ _ and his brother Andrew. (4:18)

7. "Come, you that are blessed by my Father, inherit the kingdom prepared for you from the foundation of the ❑ _ _ _ _." (25:34)

8. Matthew's Gospel is full of stories called _ _ _ _ _ _ _ ❑, which Jesus told. (13:3)

9. "_ ❑ _ _ to me, all you that are weary and are carrying heavy burdens, and I will give you rest." (11:28)

10. "You shall love the Lord your God with all your heart, and with all your soul, and with all your mind. This is the greatest and ❑ _ _ _ _ commandment." (22:37-38)

11. "Be _ _ _ _ _ _ ❑, therefore, as your heavenly Father is _____." (5:48)

12. Jesus taught as one having _ _ _ ❑ _ _ _ _ _. (7:29)

13. "Woe to you, scribes and Pharisees, hypocrites! For you lock people out of the kingdom of _ _ _ _ ❑ _." (23:13)

14. Many of the parables begin: "The ❑ _ _ _ _ _ _ of heaven is like...." (13:24,31,33)

15. The righteous will have eternal _ ❑ _ _. (25:46)

16. Both John the Baptist and Jesus proclaimed this message: "_ _ _ _ ❑ _, for the kingdom of heaven has come near." (3:2; 4:17)

17. "Then the _ _ ❑ _ _ _ _ _ _ will shine like the sun in the kingdom of their Father." (13:43)

18. "And this _ _ _ ❑ news of the kingdom will be proclaimed throughout the world, as a testimony to all the nations." (24:14)

19. "If any want to become my followers, let them deny themselves and take up their _ _ ❑ _ _ and follow me." (16:24)

20. The "Great Commission" ends with these words: "And, _ _ _ _ ❑ _ _ _, I am with you always, to the end of the age." (28:20)

❑❑❑❑ ❑❑❑❑ ❑❑ ❑❑❑

❑❑❑❑❑❑❑

Answer Key to **MATTHEW**

1. <u>G</u>ENEALOGY
2. J<u>O</u>SEPH
3. BEL<u>O</u>VED
4. BLESSE<u>D</u>
5. SO<u>N</u>
6. P<u>E</u>TER
7. <u>W</u>ORLD
8. PARABLE<u>S</u>
9. C<u>O</u>ME
10. <u>F</u>IRST
11. PERFEC<u>T</u>
12. AUT<u>H</u>ORITY
13. HEAV<u>E</u>N
14. <u>K</u>INGDOM
15. L<u>I</u>FE
16. REPE<u>N</u>T
17. RI<u>G</u>HTEOUS
18. GOO<u>D</u>
19. CR<u>O</u>SS
20. REME<u>M</u>BER

GOOD NEWS OF THE KINGDOM

MARK

A central event in the life of Jesus, as Mark tells his story, will be revealed at the bottom of this page by finding the missing words in the clues (NRSV), taking the letters from the boxes, and spelling these out below.

1. This gospel opens with all the people going out to John to be _ _ _ ☐ _ _ _ _ by him in the Jordan River. (1:4-5)
2. In those days Jesus came from _ _ _ ☐ _ _ _ of Galilee. (1:9)
3. In the wilderness for forty days, Jesus was tempted by _ ☐ _ _ _. (1:13)
4. After John was arrested, Jesus came to Galilee, proclaiming the good ☐ _ _ _ of God. (1:14)
5. ☐ _ _ _ _ and his brother Andrew were fishermen when they first saw Jesus. (1:16)
6. Jesus said to them, "☐ _ _ _ _ _ me and I will make you fish for people." (1:17)
7. As Jesus went throughout _ _ _ ☐ _ _ _ , he proclaimed the message in the synagogues and cast out demons. (1:39)
8. On the sabbath he began to teach in the _ _ _ _ ☐ _ _ _ _, and many who heard him were astounded. (6:2)
9. The sabbath was made for _ ☐ _ _ _ _ _ _ _, and not _____ for the Sabbath. (2:27)
10. With many such _ _ ☐ _ _ _ _ _ he spoke the word to them. (4:33)
11. The Son of Man is to be betrayed into human hands, and they will kill him, and three days after being killed, he will rise ☐ _ _ _ _. (9:31)
12. Then he entered Jerusalem and went into the ☐ _ _ _ _ _. (11:11)
13. Pilate, wishing to satisfy the crowd,...after flogging Jesus, handed him over to be _ _ _ _ ☐ _ _ _ _. (15:15)
14. When Jesus had breathed his last, the centurion said, "Truly, this man was God's _ ☐ _." (15:39)
15. When the sabbath was over, Mary _ _ _ _ _ _ _ ☐ _ , when the sun had risen, went to the tomb. (16:1-2)

☐ ☐ ☐ ☐ ☐ ☐ ☐ ☐ ☐ ☐ ☐ ☐ ☐ ☐

Answer Key to **MARK**

BAP<u>T</u>IZED
NAZA<u>R</u>ETH
S<u>A</u>TAN
<u>N</u>EWS
<u>SI</u>MON
<u>F</u>OLLOW
GAL<u>I</u>LEE
SYNA<u>G</u>OGUE
H<u>U</u>MANKIND
PA<u>R</u>ABLES
<u>A</u>GAIN
<u>T</u>EMPLE
CRUC<u>I</u>FIED
S<u>O</u>N
MAGDALE<u>N</u>E

TRANSFIGURATION

148

LUKE

To discover a favorite theme of evangelist Luke, select the correct bold-faced word, then take the underscored letter of that correct word to fill in the spaces at the bottom of this page in order.

1. Does Luke tell about shepherds who **GLORI̲FY** God or wise men who **PRES̲ENT** gifts?
2. In the synoptic Gospels, does Luke alone refer to Jesus as the **SAV̲IOR** or the **C̲HRIST**?
3. Did the voice at the Transfiguration tell the disciples to **L̲ISTEN** to Jesus or to **F̲OLLOW** him?
4. Does Luke locate Jesus' famous sermon on a **MOU̲NT** or a **P̲LAIN**?
5. In Luke, when Jesus enters Jerusalem, do the people throw **PALM̲S** or their **ROB̲ES** on the road?
6. Do the disciples on the way to Emmaus recognize Jesus by touching his **WOU̲ND** in the breaking of **BREA̲D**?
7. In all three synoptic Gospels, do the parables of the kingdom begin with that of the **SOW̲ER** or the **YEAS̲T**?
8. Does Pilate declare three times that Jesus has been **BE̲TRAYED** or that he is **I̲NNOCENT**?
9. Does Jesus rebuke unclean spirits because **EXO̲RCISMS** were impressive or because he had **AUT̲HORITY** to do so?
10. Does Jesus predict his death **THREE** or **SE̲VEN** times?
11. Were the religious authorities most concerned over Jesus' healings in **GAL̲ILEE** or on the **SABBAT̲H**?
12. In Luke's description of the Last Supper, does Jesus offer the cup **BOT̲H** before and after the bread or **ONL̲Y** after the bread?
13. On the first day of the week, after the crucifixion, did Cleopas and another disciple see Jesus in the **GARDE̲N** or near **EMMAUS**?
14. Is Luke's story of Lazarus the one where he's **BR̲OUGHT** back to life or where he is in the "bosom" of **ABRAH̲AM**?
15. Was the son of Zechariah named **JOH̲N** or **JUD̲E**?
16. Does Luke's gospel account begin and end in the **TEMPL̲E** or in **HEA̲VEN**?
17. Was Zacchaeus told he would be saved **TODA̲Y** or **LAT̲ER** when he had returned the money?
18. Does Jesus withstand his temptation with the help of the **SPIRI̲T** or with **QUOTE̲S** from the Scripture?
19. Does Luke have Jesus tell the disciples in Gethsemane to **WAI̲T** or to **P̲RAY**?
20. Do the parables which speak of lost things conclude with **REJOI̲CING** or **DI̲SBELIEF**?
21. Did chief priests and scribes attempt to **FIN̲D** proof of Jesus' authority or to **T̲RAP** him with their questions?
22. Is it the **SPIRI̲T** or **SATA̲N'S** will which drives Jesus into the wilderness for forty days?
23. In Luke, does an angel minister to Jesus after the **TEMPTATIO̲N** or in **GE̲THSEMANE**?

_ _ _ _ _ _ _ _ _ _ _ _ _ _ _ _ _ _ _ _ _ _ _

149

GLORI<u>F</u>Y
SAV<u>I</u>OR
<u>L</u>ISTEN
P<u>L</u>AIN
ROB<u>E</u>S
BREA<u>D</u>
SO<u>W</u>ER
<u>I</u>NNOCENT
AU<u>T</u>HORITY
T<u>H</u>REE
SABBA<u>T</u>H
BOT<u>H</u>
<u>E</u>MMAUS
ABRA<u>H</u>AM
J<u>O</u>HN
TEMP<u>L</u>E
TODA<u>Y</u>
QUOTE<u>S</u>
<u>P</u>RAY
REJO<u>I</u>CING
T<u>R</u>AP
SP<u>I</u>RIT
GE<u>T</u>HSEMANE

FILLED WITH THE HOLY SPIRIT

JOHN

After determining the missing clueword (NRSV references), fill in the squares reading across the bottom of the page. The bold-faced squares will be a phrase from the Gospel of John.

1. John's Gospel begins with the ☐ _ _ _ _ _ _ _ of John the Baptist, not with a birth story. (1:19)
2. Mary, Martha, and their beloved brother, Lazarus, were from _ _ _ ☐ _ _ _. (11:1)
3. Jesus said, "I am the true _ _ _ ☐." (15:1)
4. When John was baptizing at the Jordan, he declared Jesus to be the ☐ _ _ _ of God. (1:29,36)
5. John the Baptist denied being the Messiah and confessed himself to be the "voice of one crying out in the_ ☐ _ _ _ _ _ _ _ ." (1:23)
6. The first one to find the stone removed from the tomb was Mary _ _ ☐ _ _ _ _ _. (20:1)
7. The Passover crowd entering Jerusalem waved palm branches and shouted, "☐ _ _ _ _ _ _!" (12:12-13)
8. Jesus said, "I am the _ _ ☐ _ for the sheep." (10:7)
9. During a festival in Jerusalem, the Jews began persecuting Jesus because he was healing on the ☐ _ _ _ _ _ _. (5:10)
10. Jesus said, "I am the good ☐ _ _ _ _ _ _." (10:11)
11. _ ☐ _ _ _ _ _ _ _ was a Pharisee who came to Jesus by night and had a discussion about rebirth. (3:1)
12. Jesus responded to his mother's request while at a wedding in _ _ ☐ _. (2:1-4)
13. Jesus charged the disciples, "If you _ _ _ ☐ me, you will keep my commandments." (14:15)
14. The _ _ _ ☐ _ _ _ _ is the Jewish festival of especial importance in John's Gospel (2:13; 11:55; 12:1; 13:1)
15. Jesus said, "I am the _ ☐ _ _ _ of the world." (8:12)
16. "This is my commandment, that you love one _ ☐ _ _ _ _ _ as I have loved you." (15:12)
17. In John's Gospel, Jesus drove out the money changers then said, "Destroy this ☐ _ _ _ _ _, and in three days I will raise it up." (2:19)
18. The inscription Pilate had put above the cross in Hebrew, Greek, and Latin read: "Jesus of _ _ _ _ _ _ _ ☐, the King of the Jews". (19:19-20)
19. The only "miracle" recorded in all four gospel accounts is the feeding of the large crowd. In all four versions, there are _ _ ☐ _ _ _ baskets of bread left over. (6:13)
20. The poetic prologue of John: "In the beginning was the_ _ _ ☐, and the _ _ _ _ was with God." (1:1)
21. Jesus said, "I am the_ ☐ _, and the truth, and the life." (14:6)
22. Jesus said, "The _ _ _ _ ☐ that I will give will become in them a spring of _ _ _ gushing up to eternal life." (4:14)
23. The good shepherd said, "I ☐ _ _ _ my own and my own _ _ _ _ me." (10:14)
24. At Jacob's well, Jesus had a very long conversation with a Samaritan _ _ _ _ ☐. (4:5-39)
25. After feeding the thousands, Jesus said, "I am the _ _ ☐ _ _ of life." (6:35)
26. After Andrew met Jesus, he told his brother, Simon Peter, they had found the _ _ _ ☐ _ _ _. (1:40-41)
27. Jesus charge to Simon, "Feed my ☐ _ _ _ _." (21:17)

☐☐☐ ☐☐☐☐☐

☐☐☐☐☐☐

☐☐ ☐☐☐ ☐☐☐☐☐☐☐☐

Answer Key to **JOHN**

<u>T</u>ESTIMONY
BE<u>T</u>HANY
VIN<u>E</u>
<u>L</u>AMB
W<u>I</u>LDERNESS
MA<u>G</u>DALENE
<u>H</u>OSANNA
GA<u>T</u>E
<u>S</u>ABBATH
S<u>H</u>EPHERD
N<u>I</u>CODEMUS
CA<u>N</u>A
LOV<u>E</u>
PAS<u>S</u>OVER
L<u>I</u>GHT
A<u>N</u>OTHER
<u>T</u>EMPLE
NAZARET<u>H</u>
TW<u>E</u>LVE
WOR<u>D</u>
W<u>A</u>Y
WATE<u>R</u>
<u>K</u>NOW
WOMA<u>N</u>
BR<u>E</u>AD
MES<u>S</u>IAH
<u>S</u>HEEP

THE LIGHT SHINES IN THE DARKNESS

ACTS of the APOSTLES

To find the message, which is one of the important themes of the book of Acts, solve each clue (NRSV references), then take the boxed letters to place in the blanks below.

1. In Jerusalem, there were debates over the need for ❑ _ _ _ _ _ _ _ _ _ _.(15:1)
2. After Peter's sermon on Pentecost, three _ _ ❑ _ _ _ _ _ were baptized. (2:41)
3. On the day of _ _ ❑ _ _ _ _ _ the apostles were filled with the Holy Spirit. (2:1)
4. The first Christian martyr was ❑ _ _ _ _ _, who was stoned to death. (7:59)
5. To replace Judas as a witness to the resurrection, the apostles cast lots, and it fell to _ _ _ ❑ _ _ _ _ to become one of the twelve. (1:26)
6. When imprisoned by King Herod, an ❑ _ _ _ _ freed Peter from prison. (12:7)
7. Preceding the book of Acts is the gospel of _ _ _ ❑.
8. After Peter's vision, he realized that God shows no _ _ _ _ _ _ _ _ ❑ _. (10:34)
9. The Acts of the Apostles was written by ❑ _ _ _.
10. A dealer of purple cloth named _ ❑ _ _ _ was baptized by Paul. (16:14-15)
11. A heavenly light blinded Saul, and a voice spoke to him while he was headed to ❑ _ _ _ _ _ _ _. (9:3)
12. The gift of the Holy Spirit was poured out on _ _ _ _ _ _ ❑ _, after Peter met Cornelius. (10:45)
13. In Antioch, Paul spoke the words of Isaiah: "I have set you to be a light for the Gentiles, so that you may bring _ _ _ ❑ _ _ _ _ _ to the ends of the earth." (13:47)
14. The book of Acts ends with Paul in _ ❑ _ _. (28:16)
15. Jews in Damascus plotted to kill Saul; he escaped in a _ _ _ _ _ ❑ lowered through the wall. (9:23-25)
16. Once during a lengthy "sermon" by Paul, ❑ _ _ _ _ _ _ _ fell asleep in a windowsill and plunged three storeys to his death, but Paul brought him back to life. (20:7-12)
17. On a dangerous voyage to Italy, after being lost in a storm and shipwrecked, Paul was bitten by a viper on his _ _ _ ❑. (28:3)
18. Peter prayed for ❑ _ _ _ _ _ _ to rise from the dead. (9:36-41)
19. Following the book of Acts is the letter to the _ ❑ _ _ _ _.
20. An Ethiopian eunuch was _ _ ❑ _ _ _ _ by Philip. (8:38)
21. The story in Acts begins in _ _ ❑ _ _ _ _ _. (1:12)
22. Leaving Antioch and arriving in Cypress, Saul began to be known as _ ❑ _ _. (13:9)
23. Saul, "breathing threats and murder", sought those of the _ _ ❑. (9:1-2)
24. Paul and Silas were loosed from prison bars by an ❑ _ _ _ _ _ _ _ _, when at Philippi. (16:25-26)
25. While in a trance, Peter envisioned a sheet lowered from heaven, filled with all kinds of _ _ _ _ _ _ ❑ _ _. (10:9-16)

❑❑❑❑❑❑❑❑❑ ❑❑❑❑❑❑
❑❑ ❑❑❑❑❑

153

Answer Key to **ACTS of the APOSTLES**

<u>C</u>IRCUMCISION
TH<u>O</u>USAND
PE<u>N</u>TECOST
<u>S</u>TEPHEN
MAT<u>T</u>HIAS
<u>A</u>NGEL
JOH<u>N</u>
PARTIALI<u>T</u>Y
<u>L</u>UKE
L<u>Y</u>DIA
<u>D</u>AMASCUS
GENTIL<u>E</u>S
SAL<u>V</u>ATION
R<u>O</u>ME
BASKE<u>T</u>
<u>E</u>UTYCHUS
HAN<u>D</u>
<u>T</u>ABITHA
R<u>O</u>MANS
BA<u>P</u>TIZED
JE<u>R</u>USALEM
P<u>A</u>UL
WA<u>Y</u>
<u>E</u>ARTHQUAKE
CREATU<u>R</u>ES

CONSTANTLY DEVOTED TO PRAYER

ROMANS

Find the clue words (NRSV translation), then fill in the spaces across using the letters from the boxes. Paul's message to the Roman congregation will appear.

1. Paul was called to be an ☐ _ _ _ _ _ _. (1:1)
2. Paul was eager to proclaim the _ _ _ _ ☐. (1:15)
3. Doers of the ☐ _ _ are justified (2:13)
4. We are to live by _ ☐ _ _ _. (1:17)
5. The recipients of this letter lived in ☐ _ _ _. (1:7)
6. If you judge others, you _ _ _ _ ☐ _ _ yourself. (2:1)
7. The ☐ _ _ _ were first entrusted with God's oracles. (3:2)
8. What has now been disclosed is _ _ _ _ _ _ _ ☐ _ _ _ _ _. (3:21,22,25)
9. The ☐ _ _ _ _ _ _ dwells in us. (8:9)
10. The purpose of God's kindness to us is _ _ _ _ _ ☐ _ _ _ _. (2:4)
11. If one is debased, one deserves to _ ☐ _. (1:32)
12. Grace is a _ _ ☐ _. (3:24)
13. Law gives us knowledge of _ ☐ _. (3:20)
14. Eternal life is the ☐ _ _. (6:22)
15. When God is not acknowledged, _ _ _ _ _ ☐ _ _ _ _ fills the ungodly. (1:29)
16. _ ☐ _ _ _ _ _ was righteous for his belief in God. (4:3)
17. Paul urged the Romans to join him in _ _ _ ☐ _ _ earnestly. (15:30)
18. Abraham is _ _ _ ☐ _ _ to us all. (4:16)
19. Abraham grew strong in _ _ ☐ _ _. (4:20)
20. The God of peace will crush ☐ _ _ _ _. (16:20)
21. The revelation was kept secret for _ _ _ ☐ ages. (16:25)
22. The law brings _ ☐ _ _ _. (4:15)
23. Real circumcision is a matter of the _ _ ☐ _ _ (2:29)
24. We'll be united with Christ in the _ _ _ _ _ _ _ ☐ _ _ _ _. (6:5)
25. From Adam to Moses, _ ☐ _ _ _ exercised dominion. (5:14)
26. Jesus' blood acted as a _ ☐ _ _ _ _ _ _ _. (3:25)
27. We join Christ as _ _ _ _ ☐. (8:17)
28. Baptism is into _ _ ☐ _ _. (6:3)
29. Paul wants us to do ☐ _ _ _. (7:19)
30. For from _ ☐ _ and through _ _ _ and to _ _ _ are all things (11:36)
31. What justifies us is ☐ _ _ _ _. (3:28)
32. What Paul speaks is _ _ _ ☐ _. (9:1)

☐☐☐ ☐☐☐ ☐☐☐☐☐☐☐☐ ☐☐
☐☐☐ ☐☐☐☐☐ ☐☐ ☐ ☐☐☐☐

155

Answer Key to **ROMANS**

<u>A</u>POSTLE
GOSPE<u>L</u>
<u>L</u>AW
F<u>A</u>ITH
<u>R</u>OME
CON<u>DE</u>MN
<u>J</u>EWS
RIGHTE<u>OU</u>SNESS
<u>S</u>PIRIT
REPEN<u>T</u>ANCE
D<u>IE</u>
GI<u>F</u>T
S<u>I</u>N
<u>E</u>ND
WICKE<u>D</u>NESS
A<u>B</u>RAHAM
PRA<u>Y</u>ER
FAT<u>HE</u>R
FA<u>I</u>TH
S<u>A</u>TAN
LON<u>G</u>
W<u>R</u>ATH
HE<u>A</u>RT
RESURRE<u>C</u>TION
D<u>E</u>ATH
S<u>A</u>CRIFICE
HEIR<u>S</u>
DE<u>A</u>TH
<u>G</u>OOD
H<u>I</u>M
<u>F</u>AITH
TRU<u>T</u>H

ALL ARE JUSTIFIED BY HIS GRACE AS A GIFT

FIRST CORINTHIANS

To find one of Paul's messages to the Corinthians, find the missing words for each clue (NRSV translation). Then, take the letters in the squares to fill in the message below.

1. Paul was called to be an apostle by the ☐ _ _ _ of God. (1:1)
2. Chloe's people had reported there were _ _ _ _ _ ☐ _ _ among them. (1:11)
3. For those saved, the message of the cross is the ☐ _ _ _ _ of God. (1:18)
4. For those _ _ ☐ _ _ _ _ _ _, the message of the cross is foolishness. (1:18)
5. Let the one who ____(s), _ ☐ _ _ _ in the Lord. (1:31)
6. For I decided to know nothing among you except Jesus Christ, and him
    ☐ _ _ _ _ _ _ _ _. (2:2)
7. Because the Corinthians are spiritually immature ("infants in Christ"), Paul
    calls them "people of the _ ☐ _ _ _". (3:1)
8. After Paul had organized the Corinthian ministries, ☐ _ _ _ _ _ _ stayed and
    ministered to them. (3:6)
9. It is the _ _ ☐ _ _ _ who reveals things, searches everything, comprehends God,
    teaches us, and interprets spiritual things. (2:13)
10. God's _ _ ☐ _ _ _ is holy, and you are that ____. (3:17)
11. For our _ _ _ ☐ _ _ _ lamb, Christ, has been sacrificed. (5:7)
12. Paul warned that wrongdoers will not _ _ ☐ _ _ _ _ the kingdom of God. (6:9)
13. God will not let you be tested beyond your _ _ ☐ _ _ _ _ _. (10:13)
14. Do _ _ _ _ _ _ _ ☐ _ _ for the glory of God. (10:31)
15. Paul gave instructions concerning the Lord's ☐ _ _ _ _ _. (11:20-29)
16. Paul urged the Corinthians to be _ _ _ ☐ _ _ _ _ _ of him, as he is of Christ.
    (11:1)
17. Now you are the body of ☐ _ _ _ _ _. (12:27)
18. There are varieties of gifts, but the same _ _ _ ☐ _ _. (12:4)
19. When I became an _ _ ☐ _ _, I put an end to childish ways. (13:11)
20. Paul referred to himself as the least of all apostles, because he had
    _ _ _ _ _ ☐ _ _ _ _ the church of God. (15:9)
21. Love bears all _ _ ☐ _ _ _, believes all ____, hopes all ____, endures all ____.
    (13:7)
22. ☐ _ _ _, hope, and love abide, these three; and the greatest of these is love.
    (13:13)
23. In fact Christ has been _ _ ☐ _ _ _ from the dead, the first fruits of those who
    have died. (15:20)
24. The last enemy to be destroyed is _ ☐ _ _ _. (15:26)
25. Love never _ _ ☐ _. (13:8)

☐☐ ☐☐☐☐☐☐☐ ☐☐☐☐☐☐
☐☐☐☐☐☐☐☐☐

157

Answer Key to **FIRST CORINTHIANS**

<u>W</u>ILL
QUARR<u>E</u>LS
<u>P</u>OWER
PE<u>R</u>ISHING
B<u>O</u>AST
<u>C</u>RUCIFIED
FL<u>E</u>SH
<u>A</u>POLLOS
SP<u>I</u>RIT
TE<u>M</u>PLE
PAS<u>C</u>HAL
IN<u>H</u>ERIT
ST<u>R</u>ENGTH
EVERYTH<u>I</u>NG
<u>S</u>UPPER
IMI<u>T</u>ATORS
<u>C</u>HRIST
SP<u>I</u>RIT
AD<u>U</u>LT
PERSE<u>C</u>UTED
TH<u>I</u>NGS
<u>F</u>AITH
RA<u>I</u>SED
D<u>E</u>ATH
EN<u>D</u>S

WE PROCLAIM CHRIST CRUCIFIED

GALATIANS

There is no question about the authorship of this letter from Paul, which begins uncharacteristically not with thanksgiving for the recipients but with astonishment. Find the missing words for each clue (NRSV). Then, place the boxed letters in the spaces below to reveal one of Paul's important messages.

1. Paul considered himself an apostle sent not by _ _ _ ❑ _ authority. (1:1)
2. Paul wrote against any who would pervert the _ _ _ _ _ ❑. (1:7)
3. Paul received the gospel through a _ _ _ _ ❑ _ _ _ _ _ of Jesus Christ. (1:12)
4. Paul believed _ ❑ _ had set him apart before birth. (1:15)
5. A person is justified through ❑ _ _ _ _ in Jesus Christ. (2:16)
6. Paul's early life was characterized by violent persecutions as he tried to _ _ _ _ _ _ ❑ the church of God. (1:13)
7. Paul believed Cephas and Barnabas had been led astray by _ _ _ ❑ _ _ _ _ _. (2:13)
8. Paul had advanced in Judaism because he was more _ _ _ _ _ ❑ _ for tradition. (1:14)
9. It was _ _ _ ❑ _ _ _ whose belief in God was reckoned as righteousness. (3:6)
10. Paul's typical salutation was: "_ ❑ _ _ _ to you and peace from God our Father and the Lord Jesus Christ." (1:3)
11. Paul's call was to proclaim God's Son to the _ ❑ _ _ _ _ _ _. (1:16)
12. A person is not justified by the _ ❑ _ _ _ of law. (2:16)
13. In Christ Jesus, you are all _ _ _ _ _ _ _ ❑ of God through faith. (3:26)
14. For through the law I _ _ ❑ _ to the law, so that I might live to God. (2:19)
15. Paul accused the Galatians of being _ _ _ _ ❑ _ _. (3:1,3)
16. There is no longer Jew or Greek, there is no longer slave or free, there is no longer male and female; for all of you are _ ❑ _ in Christ. (3:28)
17. Peter was the apostle to the _ _ _ ❑ _ _ _ _ _ _ . (2:8)
18. The law was our disciplinarian until _ ❑ _ _ _ _ came. (3:24)
19. For _ ❑ _ _ _ _ _ Christ has set us free. (5:1)
20. So you are no longer a slave but a child, and if a child then also an _ _ ❑ _, through God. (4:7)
21. May I never boast of anything except the _ _ _ ❑ _ of our Lord Jesus Christ. (6:14)
22. The fruit of the _ _ _ _ _ ❑ is love, joy, peace, patience, kindness, generosity, faithfulness, gentleness and self-control. (5:22-23)

❑❑❑ ❑❑ ❑❑❑ ❑❑❑
❑❑❑ ❑❑ ❑❑❑❑❑❑

159

Answer Key to **GALATIANS**

HUM<u>A</u>N
GOSPE<u>L</u>
REVE<u>L</u>ATION
G<u>O</u>D
<u>F</u>AITH
DESTRO<u>Y</u>
HYP<u>O</u>CRISY
ZEALO<u>U</u>S
ABR<u>A</u>HAM
G<u>R</u>ACE
G<u>E</u>NTILES
W<u>O</u>RKS
CHILDRE<u>N</u>
DI<u>E</u>D
FOOL<u>I</u>SH
O<u>N</u>E
CIR<u>C</u>UMCISED
C<u>H</u>RIST
F<u>R</u>EEDOM
HE<u>I</u>R
CRO<u>S</u>S
SPIRI<u>T</u>

ALL OF YOU ARE ONE IN CHRIST

EPHESIANS

Find the missing word for each verse (NRSV clues), then take the boxed letter to spell out Paul's message at the bottom of this page.

1. ☐ _ _ _ _ _ _ be the God and Father of our Lord Jesus Christ. (1:3)
2. He chose us to be _ _ _ ☐ and blameless before him in love. (1:4)
3. Freely bestowed on us in the Beloved is his glorious ☐ _ _ _ _. (1:6)
4. In him we have ☐ _ _ _ _ _ _ _ _ through his blood. (1:7)
5. He destined us for ☐ _ _ _ _ _ _ _ as his children. (1:5)
6. In Christ we have obtained an _ _ _ _ _ _ _ _ ☐ _. (1:11)
7. You were marked with the _ ☐ _ _ of the promised Holy Spirit. (1:13)
8. I do not cease to give thanks for ☐ _ _. (1:16)
9. I remember _ ☐ _ in my prayers. (1:16)
10. When we were dead _ _ _ _ ☐ _ _ our trespasses, God made us alive together with Christ. (2:5)
11. God raised us up with Christ and seated us with him in the ☐ _ _ _ _ _ _ _ places. (2:6)
12. Through him both of us have ☐ _ _ _ _ _ in one Spirit to the Father. (2:18)
13. The mystery was made known to me by _ _ ☐ _ _ _ _ _ _ _. (3:3)
14. The Gentiles have become fellow _ ☐ _ _ _. (3:6)
15. Of this gospel I have ☐ _ _ _ _ _ a servant. (3:7)
16. Therefore be imitators of God as _ ☐ _ _ _ _ _ children, and live in love. (5:1)
17. Be subject to one another out of _ ☐ _ _ _ _ _ _ for Christ. (5:21)
18. Do not let the _ _ ☐ go down on your anger. (4:26_
19. Be ☐ _ _ _ _ _ in the Lord and in the strength of his power. (6:10)
20. Put on the whole ☐ _ _ _ _ of God. (6:11)
21. Take the shield of faith, with which you will be able to quench all the flaming arrows of the _ ☐ _ _ one. (6:16)
22. Pray in the Spirit at all times, in ☐ _ _ _ _ prayer and supplication. (6:18)
23. Grace be with all who have an _ _ ☐ _ _ _ _ love for our Lord Jesus Christ. (6:24)

☐☐ ☐☐☐☐☐ ☐☐☐

☐☐☐☐ ☐☐☐☐

☐☐☐☐☐

(Eph. 2:5)

Answer Key to EPHESIANS

1. <u>B</u>LESSED
2. HOL<u>Y</u>
3. <u>G</u>RACE
4. <u>R</u>EDEMPTION
5. <u>A</u>DOPTION
6. INHERITAN<u>C</u>E
7. S<u>E</u>AL
8. <u>Y</u>OU
9. Y<u>O</u>U
10. THRO<u>U</u>GH
11. <u>H</u>EAVENLY
12. <u>A</u>CCESS
13. RE<u>V</u>ELATION
14. H<u>E</u>IRS
15. <u>B</u>ECOME
16. B<u>E</u>LOVED
17. R<u>E</u>VERENCE
18. SU<u>N</u>
19. <u>S</u>TRONG
20. <u>A</u>RMOR
21. E<u>V</u>IL
22. <u>E</u>VERY
23. UN<u>D</u>YING

BY GRACE YOU HAVE BEEN SAVED

162

COLOSSIANS

Complete the missing words in each verse (clues are from the NRSV), then take the boxed letter to fill in the message at the bottom, which tells exactly how Christ set aside the record of our trespasses.

1. Whatever you do, in word or deed, do everything in the ❑ _ _ _ of the Lord Jesus. (3:17)
2. So if you have been raised with Christ, seek the things that are ❑ _ _ _ _. (3:1)
3. Christ is the image of the ❑ _ _ _ _ _ _ _ _ God, the firstborn of all creation. (1:15)
4. Let the word of Christ _ _ _ _ ❑ in you richly. (3:16)
5. We have not ceased _ _ _ _ ❑ _ _ for you. (1:9)
6. The Father has rescued us from the power of _ _ _ _ ❑ _ _ _. (1:12-13)
7. With ❑ _ _ _ _ _ _ _ _ in your hearts sing psalms and hymns. (3:16)
8. I, Paul, write this greeting with my own hand. Remember my _ _ _ ❑ _ _. (4:18)
9. ❑ _ _ _ _ and admonish one another in all wisdom. (3:16)
10. You were buried with him in _ _ _ ❑ _ _ _. (2:12)
11. Children, ❑ _ _ _ your parents in everything for it is your acceptable duty to the Lord. (3:20)
12. Let the peace of Christ rule in your _ _ _ _ ❑ _. (3:15)
13. Love binds everything together in perfect ❑ _ _ _ _ _ _. (3:14)
14. Christ is the _ ❑ _ _ of the body, the church. (1:18)
15. Above all, ❑ _ _ _ _ _ yourselves with love. (3:14)
16. You were also ❑ _ _ _ _ _ with him through faith. (2:12)
17. Fathers, do not _ _ ❑ _ _ _ _ your children, or they may lose heart. (3:21)
18. I am now rejoicing in my ❑ _ _ _ _ _ _ _ _ for your sake. (1:24)
19. For in him all the _ _ _ _ _ _ _ ❑ of God was pleased to dwell. (1:19)

❑❑❑❑❑❑❑ ❑❑ ❑❑
❑❑❑ ❑❑❑❑❑

Answer Key to **COLOSSIANS**

<u>N</u>AME
<u>A</u>BOVE
<u>I</u>NVISIBLE
DWEL<u>L</u>
PRAY<u>I</u>NG
DARK<u>N</u>ESS
<u>G</u>RATITUDE
CHA<u>I</u>NS
T<u>E</u>ACH
BAP<u>T</u>ISM
<u>O</u>BEY
HEAR<u>T</u>S
<u>H</u>ARMONY
H<u>E</u>AD
<u>C</u>LOTHE
<u>R</u>AISED
PR<u>O</u>VOKE
<u>S</u>UFFERINGS
FULLNES<u>S</u>

NAILING IT TO THE CROSS

FIRST THESSALONIANS

Believed to be the oldest book in the New Testament, Paul's first letter to the Thessalonians gives us a glimpse into the life of a first century church. Find the missing words (NRSV clues), then take the boxed letters from each to spell out below God's will for us (4:3).

1. The greeting identifies three senders: Paul, Timothy, and ❑ _ _ _ _ _ _ _ . (1:1)
2. A typical Pauline salutation: Grace to you and _ _ ❑ _ _ . (1:1)
3. Following the opening greetings, Paul usually gives _ _ _ ❑ _ _ for those whom he addresses. (1:2)
4. Paul claims he was as gentle with his converts as a nurse caring for ❑ _ _ _ _ _ _ . (2:7)
5. While Paul was in Athens, he sent ❑ _ _ _ _ _ _ to encourage the Thessalonians. (3:2)
6. Timothy returned with good news about their _ _ ❑ _ _ and love. (3:6)
7. Paul longed to see the Thessalonians ❑ _ _ _ to face. (2:17)
8. Paul's advice is for them to stand _ ❑ _ _ in the Lord. (3:8)
9. Paul admonishes them to rejoice always and pray without ❑ _ _ _ _ _ _ . (5:16-17)
10. God has not destined us for _ _ ❑ _ _ . (5:9)
11. The day of the Lord will come like a ❑ _ _ _ _ in the night. (5:2)
12. Do not quench the _ _ ❑ _ _ _ . (5:19)
13. Greet all brothers and sisters with a _ ❑ _ _ kiss. (5:26)
14. May the God of peace himself _ _ ❑ _ _ _ _ _ you entirely. (5:23)

❑ ❑ ❑ ❑ ❑ ❑ ❑ ❑ ❑ ❑ ❑ ❑ ❑ ❑

Answer Key to **FIRST THESSALONIANS**

<u>SI</u>LVANUS
PE<u>A</u>CE
THA<u>N</u>KS
<u>C</u>HILDREN
<u>T</u>IMOTHY
FA<u>I</u>TH
<u>F</u>ACE
F<u>I</u>RM
<u>C</u>EASING
WR<u>A</u>TH
<u>T</u>HIEF
SP<u>I</u>RIT
H<u>O</u>LY
SA<u>N</u>CTIFY

SANCTIFICATION

HEBREWS

In this puzzle, you will uncover the overarching theme for the book of Hebrews, which is a carefully constructed homily of scriptural examples and spiritual encouragement. Fill in the blanks for each clue (NRSV translation for references), then use the letters in the bold boxes to fill across the message below.

1. In Ch. 11's catalog of heroes, the _ _ _ _ ❑ _ _ _ _ "by faith" kept their eyes on God's promises. (11:2)
2. We are surrounded by a _ _ _ ❑ _ of witnesses who encourage us to run the race set before us. (12:1)
3. Long ago God spoke through _ _ _ ❑ _ _ _, but now God has provided his Son. (1:1-2)
4. Only for a short time was Jesus made lower than _ _ _ ❑ _ _. (2:5-9)
5. If we harden our hearts when put to the test, we will not enter ❑ _ _ _. (3:7-11)
6. Jesus is unlike the _ _ ❑ _ _ _ because his sacrifice does not need repeating. (7:26-28)
7. The first _ ❑ _ _ _ _ _ became obsolete when God provided a new one. (8:7,13)
8. Faith gives us _ _ _ _ ❑ _ _ _ _ for our hopes. (11:1)
9. _ _ _ _ _ ❑ _ _ _ _ _ _ was the order of priesthood bestowed by power rather than heredity. (7:15-17)
10. Type of love which must continue is _ _ ❑ _ _ _. (13:1)
11. Christ entered heaven rather than a _ _ _ _ _ _ _ _ ❑, a human-made copy. (9:24)
12. Christ's sacrifice was ❑ _ _ _ for all. (7:27; 9:26; 10:10)
13. We have been sanctified through this _ _ ❑ _ _ _ _ _, once for all. (10:10)
14. Christ's method for removing sin was _ _ ❑ _ _ _ _ _ _. (9:26)
15. Jesus is God's appointed ❑ _ _ _ of all things. (1:1-3)
16. We are called to imitate those who, through faith and patience, inherited _ ❑ _ _ _ _ _ _. (6:12)
17. What the heroes in Ch. 11 had was _ _ ❑ _ _.
18. The law is but a ❑ _ _ _ _ _ and not the true form. (10:1)
19. The type of covenant we have by Christ's blood is _ ❑ _ _ _ _ _. (13:20)

❑❑❑❑❑❑❑❑❑❑

❑❑ ❑❑❑❑❑❑

Answer Key to **HEBREWS**

ANC<u>E</u>STORS
CLO<u>U</u>D
PRO<u>P</u>HETS
ANG<u>E</u>LS
<u>R</u>EST
PR<u>I</u>ESTS
C<u>O</u>VENANT
ASSU<u>R</u>ANCE
MELCH<u>I</u>ZEDEK
MU<u>T</u>UAL
SANCTUAR<u>Y</u>
<u>O</u>NCE
OF<u>F</u>ERING
SA<u>C</u>RIFICE
<u>H</u>EIR
P<u>R</u>OMISES
FA<u>I</u>TH
<u>S</u>HADOW
E<u>T</u>ERNAL

SUPERIORITY OF CHRIST

I, II, and III JOHN

After solving the clues (NRSV translation), place the letters from the squares into the spaces below to uncover a message from these epistles. (The Roman numerals indicate in which of the three letters the verse is to be found.)

1. The darkness is passing away and the true _ _ ❑ _ _ is already shining. (I, 2:8)
2. Do not love the _ ❑ _ _ _ or the things in the ____. (I, 2:15)
3. If we say we have no sin, we ❑ _ _ _ _ _ _ ourselves, and the truth is not in us. (I, 1:8)
4. If we confess our sins, he who is faithful and just will _ _ _ _ ❑ _ _ our sins and cleanse us from all unrighteousness. (I, 1:9)
5. Three things testify: water, blood, and ❑ _ _ _ _ _. (I, 5:7)
6. The author refers to his listeners as "little _ _ _ ❑ _ _ _ _" throughout the letter. (I, 2:1, 12, 14, 18, 28)
7. We _ ❑ _ _ because he first loved us. (I, 4:19)
8. The commandment we have had from the beginning: "Let us _ _ ❑ _ one another." (II, vs. 5)
9. God is love, and those who _ _ _ _ ❑ in love ____ in God. (I, 4:16)

169

Answer Key to **I, II, and III JOHN**

LIGHT
WORLD
DECEIVE
FORGIVE
SPIRIT
CHILDREN
LOVE
LOVE
ABIDE

GOD IS LOVE

JUDE

The goal of this puzzle is to discover some of Jude's advice. First, solve the numbered clues with words from the NRSV translation. Then take the boxed letter from each word to fill in the message below.

1. ☐ _ _ _ _ perished in rebellion. (vs. 11)
2. This letter addressed to the _ ☐ _ _ _ _ _. (vs. 17)
3. _ _ _ ☐ _ was the brother of the author. (vs. 1)
4. These worldly opponents are devoid of the _ ☐ _ _ _ _. (vs. 19)
5. The land from which the LORD saved a people was _ _ ☐ _ _. (vs. 5)
6. The _ _ ☐ _ _ _ _ _ indulge in ungodly lusts. (vs. 18)
7. Those who are perverting God's grace are _ _ _ _ ☐ _ _ _ _. (vs. 4)
8. These _ ☐ _ _ _ _ _ _ are defiling the flesh. (vs. 8)
9. Salvation has been given to the _ _ _ _ _ ☐. (vs. 3)
10. These _ _ ☐ _ _ _ _ _ partake of the love-feast fearlessly. (vs. 12)
11. An evil that's done to the glorious ones is _ ☐ _ _ _ _ _. (vs. 8)
12. New Testament book which follows Jude is _ _ ☐ _ _ _ _ _ _ _.
13. Descendant of Adam who prophesied about unholy ones was ☐ _ _ _ _. (vs. 14)
14. What must be done to others is to ☐ _ _ _ them. (vs. 23)
15. Archangel who would not slander is _ ☐ _ _ _ _ _. (vs. 9)
16. Murderer who has been judged is _ _ _ ☐. (vs. 11)
17. Wandering _ ☐ _ _ _ were believed to be disobedient angels. (vs. 13)
18. Eternal punishment of fallen angels is _ ☐ _ _ _ _. (vs. 6)
19. What to offer the wavering is _ ☐ _ _ _. (vs. 22)
20. _ _ ☐ _ _ _ Made an error in prophecy. (vs. 11)
21. The dreamers reject _ _ _ _ ☐ _ _ _ _. (vs. 8)
22. The fellowship meal is the _ _ ☐ _ - _ _ _ _ _. (vs. 12)
23. The gift of Christ which leads to life is _ ☐ _ _ _. (vs. 21)
24. City that pursued unnatural lust was _ ☐ _ _ _. (vs. 7)
25. Build oneself up in ☐ _ _ _ _. (vs. 20)
26. Along with malcontents, ☐ _ _ _ _ _ _ _ _ are bombastic. (vs. 16)
27. With glory, majesty, and power, our God has _ _ _ _ ☐ _ _ _ _ forever. (vs. 25)
28. The author's name _ _ ☐ _ is a shortened form of Judas (*not* Iscariot).

☐☐☐☐ ☐☐☐☐☐☐☐☐☐

☐☐ ☐☐☐ ☐☐☐☐

☐☐ ☐☐☐

Answer Key to **JUDE**

<u>K</u>ORAH
B<u>E</u>LOVED
JAM<u>E</u>S
SP<u>I</u>RIT
EG<u>Y</u>PT
SC<u>O</u>FFERS
INTR<u>U</u>DERS
D<u>RE</u>AMERS
SAINT<u>S</u>
BL<u>E</u>MISHES
SL<u>A</u>NDER
RE<u>V</u>ELATION
<u>E</u>NOCH
<u>S</u>AVE
M<u>I</u>CHAEL
CA<u>IN</u>
ST<u>A</u>RS
C<u>H</u>AINS
M<u>E</u>RCY
BA<u>L</u>AAM
AUTH<u>O</u>RITY
LO<u>V</u>E-FEAST
M<u>E</u>RCY
S<u>O</u>DOM
<u>F</u>AITH
<u>GR</u>UMBLERS
AUTH<u>O</u>RITY
JU<u>D</u>E

KEEP YOURSELVES IN THE LOVE OF GOD

REVELATION

Find the words to fill in the blanks, then take the boxed letters to discover the message below, which gives a theme of this book. All references are from the NRSV translation.

1. Only the Lamb is ☐ _ _ _ _ to take the scroll. (5:9)
2. The never-ending song: "☐ _ _, ____, ____". (4:8)
3. Those who have come out of the ordeal have their robes washed white in _ _ ☐ _ _. (7:14)
4. The final word of the Holy Bible is _ ☐ _ _. (22:21)
5. ☐ _ _ _ _ will be no more. (21:4)
6. The location of John's exile was the island of _ _ _ _ ☐ _. (1:9)
7. Rome is represented as the fallen city _ _ _ ☐ _ _ _. (18:2)
8. The one on the throne held a seven-sealed _ _ _ ☐ _ _ in his right hand. (5:1)
9. After the seals are opened, the angels blow seven _ _ ☐ _ _ _ _ _. (8:2)
10. After seven plagues, seven angels are told to pour out seven_ _ ☐ _ _. (16:1)
11. When John saw another _ ☐ _ _ _ _ _ in heaven, it signaled the end of the wrath of God. (15:1)
12. Blessed is the one who ☐ _ _ _ _ aloud the words of the prophecy. (1:3)
13. The number of angels with trumpets is ☐ _ _ _ _. (8:6)
14. John's vision of heaven showed many things surrounding the _ ☐ _ _ _ _. (4:4)
15. Beside the river of life in the new city is the tree of _ ☐ _ _. (22:2)
16. Christ is the beginning and the end, the _ _ ☐ _ _ and the Omega. (22:13)

☐☐☐☐ ☐☐ ☐☐☐
☐☐☐☐☐☐☐

Answer Key to **REVELATION**

<u>W</u>ORTHY
<u>H</u>OLY
BL<u>O</u>OD
A<u>M</u>EN
<u>D</u>EATH
PATM<u>O</u>S
BAB<u>Y</u>LON
SCR<u>O</u>LL
TR<u>U</u>MPETS
BO<u>W</u>LS
P<u>O</u>RTENT
<u>R</u>EADS
<u>S</u>EVEN
T<u>H</u>RONE
L<u>I</u>FE
AL<u>P</u>HA

WHOM DO YOU WORSHIP

UNUSUAL
CELEBRATIONS

UNUSUAL CELEBRATIONS

Intergenerational events are extremely appealing and effective methods for teaching any topics, because the learning is cooperative across generations. When age groups are segregated for educational purposes, a false picture of society is the result, and competition is fostered. Cooperative learning among differing age groups is the ideal, with younger folks learning from the older, as they, in turn, grow from assisting the younger. It is, after all, how all those Biblical characters learned life's lessons!

Activities described in this chapter have been created for "booths" to be used in multigenerational events which strive to present a fair or carnival environment for particular Biblical themes. However, the stations are adaptable to become independent learning centers, if it is not possible to stage an intergenerational event.

The suggestions given illustrate possible activities to include at each station or learning center. The goal is to offer a bazaar or fair atmosphere. Ideas are provided for a *Ten Commandment Carnival*, a *Beatitude Bazaar*, *Revelation Revels*, and a *Creation Celebration*. Following the format depicted for each, you could easily adapt the idea to create your own themes, such as a *Parable Party* or a *Lord's Prayer Fair*.

Your event will be much more successful if you also provide appropriate refreshments, so ideas for cleverly-titled snacks are included within each plan. Your gathering will be more memorable if distinguished guests are invited. For example, a choir robe easily becomes the outfit for Moses to visit your *Ten Commandment Carnival* or the costume for Matthew or Luke to attend your *Beatitude Bazaar*.

The easiest method for creating each booth is to use a three-fold, table-top display board, available at office supply stores. Decorating these is dependent solely upon your imagination. Downloaded computer art offers wonderful illustrations. Be sure to include the appropriate Bible passages typed in large fonts. Have Bibles available at each booth, too, along with other necessary supplies for the activities. If very young learners will be attending the celebration, an older guide might need to be assigned to each booth; otherwise, the stations could be entirely self-guided.

Ten Commandment Carnival

Instructions

There are ten booths or learning centers for the Ten Commandment Carnival, each of which is based upon one of the ten commandments, as found in the twentieth chapter of Exodus. Write out the specific commandment from the Bible at each booth.

Each center contains at least two activities, most of which are card matching or sorting exercises that can be done individually or cooperatively. Copy the necessary word cards onto cardstock and store them in labeled envelopes attached to a display board. It is important to include an answer key so that the activities are self-correcting. Be sure to provide Bibles at each learning center. Encourage conversations amongst the participants at each station.

Refreshments for the Ten Commandment Carnival might be *Mount Sinai Soda* and *Commandment Cookies*. For the soda, choose any juice or soda and affix your own labels. For the cookies, shape logs of slice-and-bake cookies into rectangular bricks before slicing and baking. The cookies will then simulate tablets. Squeeze bottles of icing enable numerals to be written upon each tablet.

Any gray-bearded gentleman with a walking stick might portray Moses, your distinguished guest, made more realistic by wearing a robe.

Mount Sinai Soda

FIRST COMMANDMENT

I am the LORD your God, and you shall have no other gods before me.

ACTIVITY

What exactly is an "other god"? It is an IDOL! Anything that takes God's place in our hearts and minds is an IDOL. Anything other than God that we place as central in our lives is an IDOL. In the activity for this commandment center, sort the cards into the two categories for names of God or names of idols. (Provide in an envelope, printed individual cards for these concepts, for sorting.)

Names for God	Names of Idols
Creator	fame
YHWH	beauty
Elohim	addictions
Trinity	sports heroes
The Almighty	me
Heavenly Father	Nascar
Jehovah	MTV stars
Triune God	power
ABBA	money
El Shaddai	success
The Great I Am	movie stars

ACTIVITY

We usually think of each commandment with a number in front of it. The Hebrew language did not have separate numerals which stand for numbers. Instead, the letters of the Hebrew alphabet also stand for numbers—just like the Roman numerals which were actually Roman letters of their alphabet. The first ten letters of the Hebrew alphabet were their symbols for 1-10. Copy a chart of the Hebrew numerals 1-10 from an encyclopedia. Offer blank paper for practice in writing these numerals.

SECOND COMMANDMENT

You shall not take the name of the LORD in vain.

ACTIVITY

When is it okay to say, "Oh, God!"? Our expressions can be voiced or shown with hand gestures. When someone cries, "Oh, God," is it in a prayerful way, which might be shown with the hands folded reverently for prayer? Or, is it in tight-fisted anger or frustration? We should not use the name of the LORD in vain. Pay attention to the times every day that you hear the phrase, "Oh, God!" Try not to use it carelessly! The activity for this commandment center is to sort the cards between the two categories. (Provide in an envelope, the cards to sort, as well as titles, which might be shown by drawings of the two hand positions.)

Calling on the LORD in prayer	Calling on the LORD in anger
in hymns	when mad at others
in confession	at the evening news
in supplication	when annoyed
in thanksgiving	in disgust at people
in praise	after elections
in psalms	in road rage
in petition	in surprise
in prayer	when things go wrong

ACTIVITY

In reading the Bible, we discover that mountaintops are very likely places for folks to encounter God.   In the book of Exodus, God speaks to Moses on this holy mountain called Sinai; in chapter 20, the Hebrew nation hears God speak the Ten Commandments from this mountain; in chapter 24, God called the Hebrew leaders to the mountain; and, in chapter 24, Moses spends 40 days and 40 nights on Mt. Sinai! In the matching activity, match the cards naming mountains to the cards identifying the person who experienced a THEOPHANY (experience of God's presence) on that mountain.

Mountain	Event(s)
Ararat (Gen. 8)	Noah's ark landed here
Gerizim (Deut. 27:9-13)	Covenant was sealed.
Horeb (I Kings 19)	Elijah's theophany
Sinai (Ex. 24:18)	Moses' theophany
Zion (Psalm 78)	God's holy mountain
Nebo (Deut. 32:48-49)	Moses sees the Promised Land and is buried by God.
Moriah (Gen. 22 and I Chr. 3:1)	Binding of Isaac and Location of temple
Olives (Matt. 22:39-46)	Jesus' prayer

THIRD COMMANDMENT

Remember the Sabbath Day to keep it holy.

ACTIVITY

The third commandment offers something to the world that was unique and innovative in Moses' time—the idea of a Sabbath Day rest! An activity for this commandment center is sorting cards naming activities between those which could be considered "holy" from those which would be considered "worldly". What category of activities would be appropriate for keeping the Sabbath Day special?

Holy	Worldly
Sunday School	arguing
worship service	going to the mall
helping at a food pantry	fighting
praying	spending money
caring for family	yelling at someone
going to church	sports events
service to others	sleeping late

ACTIVITY

The Ten Commandments are found in the 20th chapter of Exodus. The Hebrew name for the book of Exodus is: **"*And these are the names*..."** That title ties this book to the ending of the previous book, Genesis. You can check this out by comparing Genesis 46:8 to Exodus 1:1. The Hebrew title also foreshadows a great name we will learn in chapter 3: **YHWH**!

We also learn the names of some of Moses' family in the book of Exodus. A matching activity for this commandment center is to try to pair the names of Moses' relatives with their relationship to him. (These are printed on orange colored cards and placed in an envelope for pairing.)

Aaron (Ex.4:14)	brother
Amram (Ex. 6:20)	father
Miriam (Ex. 15:20)	sister
Zipporah (Ex. 2:21)	wife
Jochebed (Ex. 6:20)	mother
Jethro (Ex. 3:1)	father-in-law
Gershom (Ex. 2:22)	son

FOURTH COMMANDMENT

Honor your Father and your Mother that your days may be long.

ACTIVITY

We learn the names of many sets of parents and children throughout the Bible. See how many of these you can match with the cards in the envelopes. The answers are on the reverse.

Parent(s)	Child(ren)
Adam & Eve	Cain & Abel
Adam & Eve	Seth
Noah	Shem, Ham, & Japheth
Abraham & Hagar	Ishmael
Abraham & Sarah	Isaac
Isaac & Rebekah	Esau & Jacob
Jacob & Rachel	Joseph
Ruth & Boaz	Obed
Jesse	David
Hannah & Elkanah	Samuel
Saul	Jonathan
David & Bathsheba	Solomon
Elizabeth & Zechariah	John the Baptist

ACTIVITY

Genealogies are important in the Hebrew Bible. Provide blank charts of a simple family tree that each participant might complete.

FIFTH COMMANDMENT

You shall not kill.

ACTIVITY

Many of us learned the Fifth Commandment as "Thou shall not kill." However, a better translation of the Hebrew is "Thou shall not murder." Sometimes we can "kill" a person's SPIRIT. Do you build someone up or tear someone down with how you act and what you say? Is killing ever allowable? The sorting card activity in the envelope might raise some questions about how to keep or break this commandment.

YES or NO?

Is it okay to hunt animals for meat or food?

Is it okay to kill snakes?

Is it okay to kill bugs inside? Outside?

Do you say cruel things?

Do you eat healthy foods? Do you exercise?

Do you drive too fast?

Should we take part in war?

Do you take drugs?

ACTIVITY

Jesus summarizes the Ten Commandments into how many? Look up these New Testament passages to see what Jesus' commandments are:
>   Matthew 22:34-40   Mark 12:28-31
>   Luke 10:25-28   John 15:12
How is it possible that Jesus' commands replace the Ten?

SIXTH COMMANDMENT

You shall not commit adultery.

ACTIVITY

Sometimes we do not know what words mean! How can we follow instructions when we cannot understand them? Adultery is a word you may not know. Think of this commandment as asking you to be LOYAL and FAITHFUL and UNSELFISH in all your relationships! The matching card activity for this commandment center shows how difficult it is to comprehend directions that we cannot read or understand. Try to match each picture of an appliance with the actual directions for its use—but these are written in foreign languages!

ACTIVITY

Another set of sorting cards for this commandment center helps you decide which actions are LOYAL and FAITHFUL and UNSELFISH in your relationships.

<u>YES or NO?</u>
Do you gossip about people?

Do you try to "buy" friendship?

Do you keep confidences people tell you?

Are you loyal to your friends?

Are you honest in your relationships?

Are you faithful in your relationships?

Do you talk behind peoples' backs?

Do you use others for your own purposes?

SEVENTH COMMANDMENT

You shall not steal.

ACTIVITY

The sorting cards activity for this commandment center requires you to decide if an action should be considered stealing.

YES or NO?

Do you cheat?

Do you waste time?

Do you use things without permission?

Do you break things out of carelessness?

Do you take things that are not yours?

Do you waste things?

Do you waste natural resources (like water)?

Do you copy things without permission?

ACTIVITY

Do you know the Ten Commandments in order? An activity for this commandment center is to see if you can match the cards with just the numbers 1 – 10 on them to the set of cards with the commandments written upon them.

EIGHTH COMMANDMENT

You shall not bear false witness.

ACTIVITY

In ancient Israel, a person could be convicted of a crime on the basis of spoken testimony alone. Is it ever okay to be untruthful? The sorting cards activity for this commandment center requires you to decide if certain actions are honest or not.

YES or NO?

Do you make excuses to get out of trouble?

Do you lie or tell half-truths?

Do you tell "stories" about yourself to look good?

Do you try to make others look foolish?

Do you spread rumors?

Do you tell "stories" to get others in trouble?

Are "white lies" okay?

Do you ignore your responsibilities to others?

ACTIVITY

Prepare cards for a sequencing activity (remembering to include an answer key) that highlights the chronology of events in the book of Exodus:

OPPRESSION
PLAGUES
PASSOVER
RED SEA CROSSING
WILDERNESS WANDERING
COVENANT AND TABLETS
PROMISED LAND

ACTIVITY

Did you know that the commandments are not actually numbered in the Bible? Sometimes the Ten Commandments are called the **DECALOGUE**, which is the Greek for "ten words". There are *ten* commandments. In reading the Bible, certain numbers show up regularly. These often have symbolic meaning. One number that occurs often is "**THREE**". It appears 639 times. Compare that to the name of "Jesus", which appears 994 times! The number "**FORTY**" appears 117 times. The number "**TEN**" makes 240 showings; the number "**TWELVE**" is used 247 times. In the sorting exercise for this commandment center, place each event under the heading for **TEN(10)** or **TWELVE (12)** according to its count in the Bible. (Have the correct answers on the backs of the cards you make.)

TEN	TWELVE
How many commandments (Deut. 4:13; 10:14)	How many loaves of bread Moses had to place on the golden table of the tabernacle (Lev. 24:5)
How many plagues in Egypt	How many disciples Jesus summoned (Mt. 10:1)
How many steps led into the temple of Ezekiel's vision (Ezek. 40:49)	How many basins of bronze in Solomon's temple (I Kgs. 7:27,38)
How many springs of water at Elim (Ex. 15:27)	How many kinds of fruit on the tree of life (Rev. 22:2)
How many horns on the beast (Rev. 13:1)	How many baskets were filled after Jesus fed the 5,000 (Mt. 14:20)
How many curtains in the tabernacle (Ex. 26:1)	How old was Jesus when his family "lost" him at the temple (Lk. 2:42)
How many lepers did Jesus heal (Lk. 17:12)	How many sons of Jacob (Gen. 35:22)
How many bridesmaids had lamps in Jesus' parable (Mt.25:1)	How many foundations in the New Jerusalem (Rev. 21:14)
How many elders heard Boaz's claim to Ruth (Ruth 4:2)	How many pillars Moses set up at base of Mt. Sinai (Ex. 24:4)
How many golden lampstands in the temple (II Chr. 4:7)	How many tribes of Israel (Gen. 49:28)

NINTH COMMANDMENT

You shall not covet your neighbor's wife.

What does covet mean? To covet something is to greedily want or desire anything belonging to someone else. The feelings of ENVY and JEALOUSY are related. Different denominations (religions) number the Ten Commandments differently! Jewish, Protestant, and Eastern Orthodox churches separate the commandments about worshipping other gods from the commandment about making idols. Roman Catholic and Lutheran churches combine the two about other gods and idols but separate the last two about things not to be coveted.

ACTIVITY

A sequencing activity for this commandment center requires you to take the commandment cards (without numbers) in the envelope and place them in the order in which we receive them in the story of Exodus.

ACTIVITY

The story of the Ten Commandments being given to Moses is found in the Old Testament book of **Exodus**. Exodus is part of the **TORAH**, or **LAW**, which is what we call the first five books of the Old Testament. Sometimes these are called the Books of Moses. All the books of the Bible are organized into sections, according to the type of writing they are. Take the cards from the envelope and see if you can order these categories in the sequence they appear in the Bible. You can check your work in the Table of Contents of a Bible. (The color-coded cards to be sequenced show the category AND list the books of the Bible in that category beneath the heading, but for convenience' sake, the names of the books are not listed in the following list.)

LAW   HISTORY
WRITINGS (POETRY)   MAJOR PROPHETS
MINOR PROPHETS   GOSPELS
HISTORY
EPISTLES (LETTERS)
APOCALYPSE

TENTH COMMANDMENT

You shall not covet your neighbor's things.

ACTIVITY

Life can be a rocky path! The Ten Commandments help us along that path to living a life with God at the center. Look on the floor at the "Stepping Stones". Walk the path they show. As you step on each stone, try to recite the commandment for that number. Or, for younger people, as someone says the name of a commandment, you step on that numbered stone. (Take ten sheets of gray cardboard, cut them roughly in the shapes of stones, and number them from 1 – 10. Lay them out on the floor in a stepping stone pattern.)

ACTIVITY

You've made it through all the commandment centers now. The naming exercise in the first envelope tests your memory. For each numbered card, try to name the commandment for it. (Have an envelope containing cards with numbers only on each, one through ten.)

ACTIVITY

For younger folks, feel free to take a Ten Commandments brochure from the envelope. This will be your own personal reminder of what the Ten Commandments are. (Have a little page listing the Ten Commandments for each child to take.)

ACTIVITY

For older folks, take a sheet of blank paper and try to rewrite the Ten Commandments for modern times as the "Ten Essential Things We Are Called to Do".

BEATITUDE BAZAAR

Instructions

There are seven booths or learning centers for the Beatitude Bazaar. Their purpose is to foster understanding of the Beatitudes as presented both in Matthew 5:1-12 and Luke 6:20-26. The activities range from those for children to those for older participants. They truly work best in a multigenerational setting.

The centers contain one or more activities which can be done individually or cooperatively. Copy any necessary card matching or card sorting activities onto cardstock and store these in labeled envelopes attached to the display board for that booth. Be sure to include answer keys so that the activities may be self-correcting. Also, provide Bibles at each learning center. Encourage conversations amongst the participants at each station.

Refreshments for the Beatitude Bazaar might be:
    Pure-in-Heart Punch
    Luke's Lemonade
    Matthew's Mini-Muffins
    Gospel Grapes
    Beatitude Brownies
Be sure to label them!

Inviting distinguished guests might add to the festivities. Sandals, robes, and rope belts are the only costuming needed for Matthew or Luke to arrive, but computer-generated business cards or nametags might be fun:

HELLO. MY NAME IS
Matthew
Best-selling author of
"The Gospel of Matthew"

Learning Center One

UPWARD BOUND

ACTIVITY

Use Bibles to look up both stories of the beatitudes:

    Matthew 5:1-12

    Luke 6:20-26

Notice the different characteristics of each. Prepare sorting cards, with the following phrases, to be divided into these two categories:

Matthew	Luke
Sermon on the Mount	Sermon on the Plain
Audience—disciples	Audience—crowd
8 beatitudes	4 beatitudes & 4 woes
"kingdom of heaven" talk	"kingdom of God" talk
3rd person	2nd person plural
spiritualized	states of being
attitudes	actions

ACTIVITY

Provide photocopied maps (see next page for map to use) for each participant, with these instructions:

    Place a yellow star on Bethlehem.

    Place red circles around Nazareth, Cana, and Capernaum.

    Place a black cross on Jerusalem.

    Place a purple "X" on the Mount of Olives.

    Shade in blue the Jordan River, the Sea of Galilee, the Dead Sea, and the Mediterranean Sea.

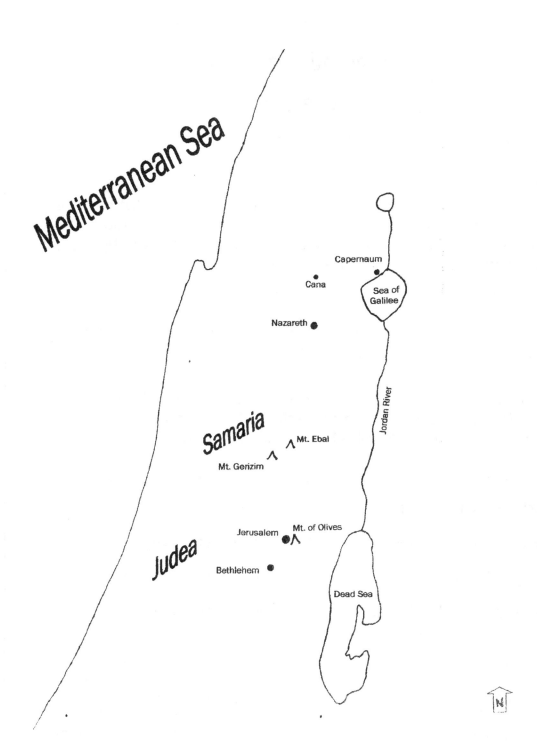

Mediterranean Sea

Capernaum

Cana

Sea of
Galilee

Nazareth

Jordan River

Samaria

Mt. Ebal

Mt. Gerizim

Jerusalem

Mt. of Olives

Judea

Bethlehem

Dead Sea

N

Learning Center Two

WOE IS ME!

ACTIVITY

Prepare a sorting exercise with cards upon which all of Matthew's eight beatitudes are written and cards upon which Luke's four beatitudes and four woes are written. The activity is to sort them between the proper Gospel accounts. Provide Bibles for checking the work.

ACTIVITY

Prepare a matching exercise with cards that have Matthew's beatitudes divided into cause and effect. The exercise is to match these correctly. Provide Bibles for checking the work.

Blessed Are...	For They Will...
Blessed are the poor in spirit	for theirs is the kingdom of heaven.
Blessed are those who mourn	for they will be comforted.
Blessed are the meek	for they will inherit the earth.
Blessed are those who hunger and thirst for righteousness	for they will be filled.
Blessed are the merciful	for they will receive mercy.
Blessed are the pure in heart	for they will see God.
Blessed are the peacemakers	for they will be called children of God.
Blessed are those who are persecuted for righteousness' sake	for theirs is the kingdom of heaven.

Learning Center Three

CONGRATULATIONS!

ACTIVITY

You will create a board game called *"Follow the Way to Kingdom Living"* to be used at this learning center when more than one participant has gathered. Materials are simply one piece of white posterboard, buttons to use for markers, and one cube of a pair of dice. Draw freehand on the posterboard a sequence of thirty "stepping stone" shapes, with the words shown below written onto each, along with the numbers and a pathway.

START
1) You know the difference between right and wrong.
2) You comfort those you see crying.
3) When people call you names, you do not call names back.
4) Sometimes you are sad, but God still loves you.
5) You forgive people who hurt you.
6) If someone hits you, you do not hit back.
7) Sometimes you need to be comforted, but God still loves you.
8) You try to stop people from fighting.
9) You stand up for people who are being bullied.
10) You look for the good in people.
11) You hug people because it will make them happy.
12) You try not to hurt people.
13) Hug the person standing to your right.
14) You look on the bright side of things.
15) Sometimes you are bullied, but you do not bully back.
16) You try to settle arguments.
17) You do not brag.
18) Switch places with the person to your left, to take another turn.
19) You do not do anything you know to be wrong.
20) If someone picks on you, you try to ignore it.
21) You always try to do the right thing.
22) Everyone playing must sing aloud "Jesus Loves Me This I Know".
23) Hug the person standing to your left.
24) You always try to help others.
25) If someone is hungry, you try to help.
26) You do not mind sharing.
27) You defend those who are weaker.
28) Sometimes you are depressed, but you know God is with you.
29) Everyone playing must sing aloud, "Jesus Loves the Little Children".
30) CONGRATULATIONS—You have found KINGDOM LIVING.

Each player rolls the die to see how many spaces to advance his button marker. The words on the place where he lands must be read aloud. All players keep going until every-one reaches "Kingdom Living". There are no losers—everybody gets there eventually!

Learning Center Four

STRANGERS in a STRANGE LAND

ACTIVITY

Have Matthew's beatitudes listed on separate cards. On another set of cards, print the following popular slogans. The exercise is to contrast the widely accepted slogans or maxims for living the "American Way" of life to the beatitudes describing "Kingdom Living", which they contradict. For example:

BLESSED ARE THE POOR IN SPIRIT

could be the opposite of

HE'S A SELF-MADE MAN

There may be more than one possible match for each card. Ideas for slogan cards include:
Might makes right.
Get off my back!
Survival of the fittest.
Go for the gold!
There's no such thing as a free lunch.
To the victor go the spoils.
Keep a stiff upper lip.
Every man for himself.
Make my day!
Looking out for number one.
My way or the highway!
He has a hidden agenda.
It's just as easy to marry a rich man.
Eat my dust.
I did it my way.
Last one there's a rotten egg!
Diamonds are a girl's best friend.
The race goes to the swift.
Hit the road, Jack.
You can't be too rich or too thin.
Take a number, buddy!

Learning Center Five

PICK KINGDOM LIVING

Beatitude is not a word you will find in an English translation of the Bible. The Greek word in the original text is an adjective, describing someone; it is not a verb conferring blessing. The Greek word translated as "woe" (from Luke) is just an interjection; it is not a curse. Maybe the French have it correct, as they translate "Blessed are…" as "Happy are…" instead.

ACTIVITY

Remember the fortune-tellers you probably folded out of square paper when you were in grade school? For this activity every participant will make a blessings-teller. You must prepare in advance pre-printed squares of paper which will then be folded at the learning center, according to the instructions provided. When the flaps are open, each spot will reveal one of the beatitudes.

The following page provides a template you may use for copying pre-printed pages for the activity. (You may wish to enlarge this.) You must cut these pages into squares before they can be folded. Following that template, you will find the instructions for folding each printed square into a blessings-teller. When preparing the activity for a booth or learning center, you may wish to have an actual example representing each stage of the folding process, to make it easier to follow.

Do you remember how they are used? A person first selects a number, which is counted, as the blessings-teller is moved back and forth. Then the person picks one of the colors. The name of the color is spelled out as the blessings-teller is moved back and forth again. Finally, the person chooses the space to be opened up to reveal his blessing.

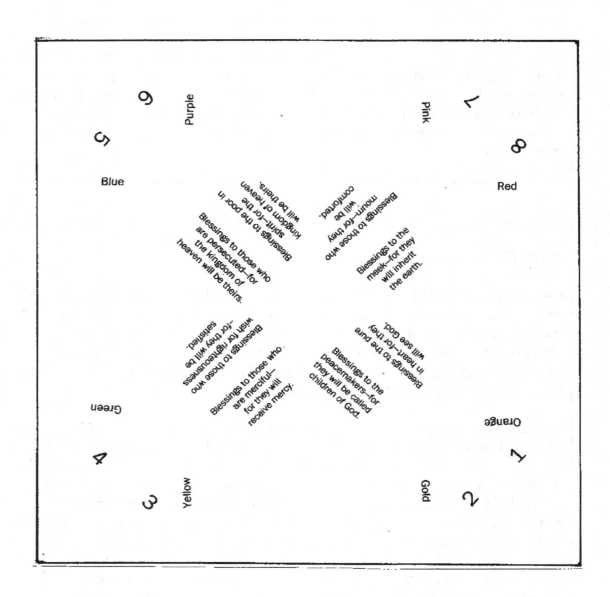

Blessings-Teller

Folding Instructions

Begin with the printing facing
up. Fold the square in half
both directions, re-opening
after each fold.

Also crease the diagonals,
re-opening after each fold.
These scored lines will be
the guides for the next steps.

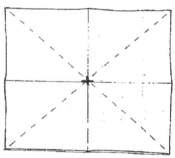

Turn the paper so the writing is
facing downward. Fold each
corner into the center, which
results in a smaller square.

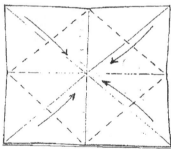

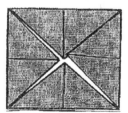

Now turn the paper over and fold the corners into the center again.

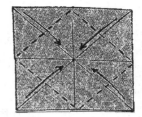

Again, turn the paper over, and you will see four square flaps. Fold piece in half, so you have two of these flaps on each outer side.

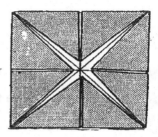

Put one of your fingers into each of these four flaps and gently press the folded points toward each other in the center, forming the completed diamond-like shape that moves back and forth as your fingers move inside.

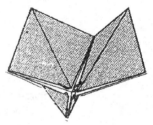

CURRICULUM VITAE

What would a job description, based upon the beatitudes, request?

+ Someone who stands empty-handed before God.

+ Someone who sympathizes with any who suffer.

+ Someone who is humble and vulnerable.

+ Someone who seeks a right relationship with God and others.

+ Someone who is open to receive mercy and forgiveness.

+ Someone who looks for the good in all things.

+ Someone who is ready to experience and to establish peace.

+ Someone who does not try to "get even" when wronged by others.

++

Are any of us able to accomplish these things alone? Not likely!

Who is able to accomplish all of these things? Jesus himself.

ACTIVITY

Have cards printed with the following events from Jesus' life on each.
The exercise is to order them correctly as they occurred. Be sure to
provide an answer key.

Baptism	Transfiguration
Temptation	Ascension
Calling the disciples	Last Supper
Sermon on the Mount	Triumphal Entry into Jerusalem

Learning Center Seven

THE KINGDOM IS . . .

ACTIVITY

At this station, participants will help to create a mural collage that depicts the kingdom of God. Have either a large piece of posterboard or a roll of mural paper (such as the end of a roll of newsprint as used by a newspaper publisher). The caption would read:

The Kingdom of God is the Presence of God

Have enough glue sticks and scissors on hand, as well as a good supply of appropriate pictures which show aspects of all creation—from glorious land, sea and cloudscapes to colorful and diverse animals of all kinds. It is equally important to find as many pictures as possible of humankind from all over the globe. Particularly excellent sources for such color pictures are "*National Geographic*" magazine, "The *Lutheran*" magazine, and periodicals and catalogs such as those sent from *Heifer International*. You might also consider taking digital photos to print of each participant, so that these may also be attached to the collage.

Each participant will contribute to the mural by selecting and placing pictures on the poster. The completed poster could then be placed on a bulletin board or central location of the facility.

REVELATION
REVELS

Instructions

Seven learning centers are created for this multigenerational celebration. Directions are provided for activities and information cards to be used at each of these stations. You might decorate your displays with artwork printed from internet sources. Also have Bibles at each booth.

For your refreshment table, you might wish to offer a selection of the following treats, including labels:

> Apocalypse Punch
> Book-of-Life Brownies
> Doxology Donuts
> Twelve-Fruit Cocktail
> Patmos Pretzels/Popcorn
> White-Robe White Chocolate Chip Cookies
> New Jerusalem Juice

John of Patmos might be a distinguished guest to your fair, costumed simply in a robe. Anachronistic props might be fun; he could have hand-cuffs (he was an exiled prisoner) or envelopes and stamps (he did write letters). He could distribute to the participants little rolled scrolls with this message inside:

| Worship God! |

Appropriate charts in this text might be copied onto your displays, also. For example, "Postings from Patmos" might be used in station one.

Learning Center One

MAIL CALL

Over 19 centuries ago, a man named John was held prisoner on the island of Patmos in the Mediterranean Sea.

One Sunday, while John was worshipping God, he had a series of strange and colorful visions. Visions are something you see in your mind's eye—like a dream, but you don't have to be asleep.

The visions showed John some truths about worshipping God.

Do you remember your dreams?

John wrote down the visions which were revealed to him, and he sent his writings to seven churches in nearby Asia Minor.

The letters were the words of Jesus Christ, who knew the churches well, and who was offering promises to them.

Do you write letters to people you know?

ACTIVITY

Prepare blank map pages for the participants. Have students draw a star at the location of each of these churches:

Ephesus
Smyrna
Pergamum
Thyatira
Sardis
Philadelphia
Laodicea

Or, you could provide a standard map and have participants locate the cities named.

ACTIVITY

It is not likely that the John who wrote the Book of Revelation is the same John we meet elsewhere in the New Testament. There are possibly five different "JOHN" characters in the New Testament. For this matching exercise, prepare cards based upon the following: (Remember to provide answer keys, so the activity might be self-directing.)

BIBLE REFERENCE	IDENTITY
Mark 1:4; 7:17-29	John who baptized people and irritated Herod
Gospel of John	John the Evangelist
John 1:42; 21:15	John, father of Simon peter
Revelation 1:9	John of Patmos, an exile
Matthew 4:21	John, fisherman and disciple, son of Zebedee and brother to James

Learning Center Two

CRAZY CRITTERS

John's visions showed terrible tragedies that have happened and do happen to people on earth.

People have died in wars, when countries battle one another.
People have lost their lives in revolts, when there is fighting.
People die from famine, when there is not enough food.
People suffer from all types of diseases and disabilities.
People suffer from disasters in the world, like storms or floods.
People suffer from cruelty by people with power.
People mourn when people they love suffer.

Whom do we worship when such terrible things happen?

In John's time, the Roman emperors wanted everyone to worship them as gods. When Christians refused, they were *persecuted*. That is, they could be put in prison and sometimes killed. Those who died this way were called *martyrs*.

Some of John's visions have scary images that warn Christians about persecution.

Do you think there is persecution today?

In Revelation, animals are often used as symbols. Some examples are:

The LION is the mightiest wild animal on earth.
The OX is the strongest domesticated animal.
The EAGLE is the mightiest winged creature.
The DRAGON stands for evil.
The SERPENT is a symbol for Satan.
The LAMB is a gentle creature used as a sacrifice.

ACTIVITY

We still use animals in modern language to stand for particular characteristics. For this exercise, have cards in an envelope which will be matched as well-known similes. Be sure to provide an answer key.

Horse	as hungry as a
Hornet	as mad as a
Rabbit	as quick as a
Mule	as stubborn as a
Clam	as happy as a
Loon	as crazy as a
Lamb	as gentle as a
Ox	as strong as an
Camel	as thirsty as a
Tiger	as fierce as a

ACTIVITY

Revelation also uses colors to mean things. For example,
    Red can mean blood, fire, or war.
    Black can mean death.
    Gold can mean royalty.
    White can mean purity or victory.

We use colors symbolically in our church liturgy, too. Each season of the church year has its own color. For this exercise, have cards prepared to match. Be sure to provide an answer key.

SEASON	COLOR	SYMBOLISM
Advent	Blue	Anticipation, hope
Christmas	White	Joy, purity, light
Epiphany	Green	Growth, nourishment
Lent	Purple	Penitence, royalty
Easter	Gold	Royalty, precious
Pentecost	Red	Fire, blood, Holy Spirit

ACTIVITY

We still use colors in our modern language to represent particular characteristics. For this exercise, have matching cards for these well known metaphors. Remember to offer an answer key.

Seeing red	Anger
White as the driven snow	Innocence
Green around the gills	Sea-sick
Yellow-bellied	Cowardly
To be golden	Lucky
Feeling blue	Melancholy
Green-eyed monster	Envy

ACTIVITY

Create a circus-style life-sized cut-out in which everyone appears as a white-robed saint. Provide a large drawing of a white-robed person with an oval opening cut out where the face would go. Have digital photos taken of the participants standing behind this with their faces peering through the cut out. If possible, print the photos instantly and give to each person.

Learning Center Three

NO ONE LEFT BEHIND

You will need to make copies of the *"No One Is Left Behind"* number charts from the *Useful Charts* chapter of this manual. These will be helpful to display within this learning center or station.

John of Patmos used numbers as part of his coded language. A code is necessary when enemies are watching what you do or say. The enemy in John's day was the Roman Empire. Remember the Roman rulers were persecuting Christians.

ACTIVITY

Prepare worksheets that show a number code to be solved to discover a hidden message. One popular code is formed by assigning a number to each letter of our alphabet. Provide a chart illustrating this:

A=1	B=2	C=3	D=4	E=5
F=6	G=7	H=8	I=9	J=10
K=11	L=12	M=13	N=14	O=15
P=16	Q=17	R=18	S=19	T=20
U=21	V=22	W=23	X=24	Y=25
Z=26				

Your coded message might be:

23 + 15 + 18 + 19 + 8 + 9 + 16   7 + 15 + 4

Learning Center Four

LUCKY SEVEN

One of the numbers which recurs regularly in Revelation is the number seven. Not only is seven used for the number of many objects named in the book, it is also used as the number of times certain phrases are mentioned in the book. And, there are lists of things that have seven items in the lists.

ACTIVITY

This is a matching activity that stresses how often seven is used. Prepare cards to be used as follows, but the irony is that every object has the same number—seven!

How Many?	Objects
Seven	Churches
Seven	Stars
Seven	Angels
Seven	Bowls
Seven	Trumpets
Seven	Lampstands
Seven	Seals

ACTIVITY

Prepare worksheets that ask participants to fill in the lists of seven-fold objects from the passages given. The correct answers are:

Rev. 5:12   What is the seven-fold praise?
(power, wealth, wisdom, might, honor, glory, and blessing)

Rev. 6:12-14   What are the seven calamities named?
(earthquakes, blackened sun, blood red moon, stars fall to earth, sky vanishes, mountains removed, and islands removed)

Rev. 6:15 Who are the seven types who wish to hide from the Lamb?
(kings of earth, magnates, generals, the rich, the powerful, slaves, and free)

Rev. 7:15-17 What is the seven-fold description of the Lamb's protection?
(shelter, no hunger, no thirst, no sunburn, no scorching heat, guided to springs of water of life, and all tears wiped away)

ACTIVITY

Lucky Seven Board Game—On a piece of poster board, make a game board that depicts a pathway of seven columns connected with arrows from start to finish. Each column will be marked by seven positions with a cut-out figure at each:

Column 1--Seven letters
Column 2--Seven angels
Column 3--Seven stars
Column 4--Seven lampstands
Column 5--Seven scrolls
Column 6--Seven angels with trumpets
Column 7--Seven angels with bowls

The goal is to follow the pathway to reach the Tree of Life. Each player selects a colored button for a marker. The play is to take turns rolling the dice. Move the button marker according to the number rolled. All players reach the Tree of Life. Everyone is a winner; there are no losers!

Learning Center Five

MARY HAD A LITTLE LAMB

John's visions show that the Lamb will deliver us from evil. Evil is doomed, because God is all powerful. God will even defeat death. God will rule forever, and all tears of suffering will be wiped away.

Do you know someone who is suffering right now?

Some suffering that John wrote about reminds us of the plagues that happened in Egypt during the time of Moses. God's people should know by heart the story of God delivering them from their suffering in Egypt. God will continue to deliver us.

Do you know the story of Moses?

John saw a scroll with seven seals closing it. Only our Lord, Jesus Christ, who is also called the Lamb, was able to open the seals.

A lamb has been a symbol of God's deliverance since the first Passover in Egypt thousands of years ago.

Jesus, the Lamb of God, has delivered us by his death on a cross.

Do you know the Passover story?

In Revelation 5:6 we meet the LAMB. Of course, we are reminded of the Passover Lamb from the 12th chapter of Exodus. Revelation uses the word "lamb" nearly 30 times to help us accept this imagery of a new Exodus, or escape from our slavery to sin, through the Lamb.

We are so used to the idea of the Lamb of God, that we might not realize that apart from John the Baptist's one comment at the beginning of The Gospel of John, in no other place in the New Testament is Jesus referred to as a Lamb.

Self-stick closures and lick-to-seal envelopes are a modern luxury. In olden times, to close a document, which might be a scroll, a seal was attached by melting wax over the closure. A king or other official might then press his ring, called a signet, into the sealing wax to make an impression that would identify him as the wax hardened.

ACTIVITY

Take a blank strip of paper and write down names of people who are suffering right now and for whom you wish prayers to be given to God. Roll up your paper strip into a cylinder shape, like a scroll, and seal it closed with one of the special stickers provided. Place your prayer request in the special box provided.

ACTIVITY

Lambs play a starring role throughout scripture. See if you can place the cards for this exercise in order, according to their appearance in the Bible. (Make cards for each item in this list. Be sure to provide an answer key.)

Gen. 4:2-7	Abel, a keeper of sheep, gave God the firstlings of his flock.
Gen. 22:1-14	Isaac, at the last minute, is saved from sacrifice by a ram (who used to be a lamb!) caught in a bush.
Exo. 12:1-13	Passover Lamb's blood on lintel kept the people safe from the angel of death passing.
Lev. 1:1-4	Sacrificial lambs as offerings are described also in the 7th & 28th chapters of this law code.
II Sam. 12:1-7	Nathan told King David a parable about a lamb, a beloved pet that lost its life.
Isa. 11:6	Isaiah foretells of the time to come when the wolf shall live with the lamb in peace.
John 1:29,36	John the Baptist identifies Jesus as the Lamb of God.
Rev. 5:6-14	John of Patmos has visions that show the Lamb on the throne.

ACTIVITY

A matching exercise is made from the following cards to show how images from the Revelation are taken directly from Old Testament passages.

Hebr. 4:12	Rev. 1:16; 19:15—Sword from mouth
Eze. 1:10	Rev. 4:6-8—Four living creatures
Zech. 6:1-7	Rev. 6:2-8—Colored horses
Ex. 10:12-15	Rev. 9:3-9—Hordes of locusts
Eze. 3:1-3	Rev. 10:8-10—Scroll eaten
Dan. 7:19-20	Rev. 13:1—Beast with horns
Ex. 7:14-24	Rev. 16:3-4—Rivers into blood
Isa. 1:12	Rev. 17—Great harlot
Jer. 15:24-64	Rev. 18—Doom of Babylon
Dan. 7:10	Rev. 20:12—Book of judgment
Eze. 41-42	Rev. 21:15-17—Temple measured
Gen. 2:9-10	Rev. 22:1-2—Tree of Life
Eze. 41-42	Rev. 22:2—Leaves of fruit tree for healing

Learning Center Six

IT'S ALL GREEK TO ME

A Ω

A is the **ALPHA**, the first letter of the alphabet. It symbolizes the beginning.

Ω is the **OMEGA**, the last letter of the Greek alphabet. It symbolizes the ending.

Our Lord Jesus is the Beginning (**the Alpha**) and the Ending (**the Omega**) of the story.

χ ρ

XP is the **CHI-RHO**.

These are the first two letters of the Greek word for Christ. It is often used as a monogram for Christ.

IHΣ

This is another popular variation of the first letters of Jesus' name. In Greek capitals, that would be IHSOUS. The Greek letters had no "J", and the "H" was our "E" sound.

ΙΧΘΥΣ

This is the Greek word for fish. As a monogram for Jesus, it originates from the first letters for five words describing Jesus:

I from Iesus (Jesus)

X from Christos (Christ)

Θ from Theos (God)

Υ from Ulios (Son)

Σ from Soter (Saviour)

ΑΠΟΚΑΛΥΨΙΣ

This Greek word, which we translate as either apocalypse or revelation, means to uncover, to reveal, or to pull back the veil. It is actually a genre of literature that was popular in Biblical times. Early examples of apocalypse may be found in the book of Daniel and in the last chapters of Ezekiel.

Basically, an apocalypse is a way for an author to warn his readers of evil without endangering the author. This is done by using an "apocalyptic tense", wherein the author takes an event from the past and predicts it as a future event, in order to warn folks about the present evil.

Characteristics of apocalypse include:

+Based upon a period of crisis or persecution

+Contrasts a present "evil" age with a heavenly age to come, in order to give the message, "Hold on!" or "Keep the faith!"

+Uses symbolism extensively

+Interpreted often by a heavenly messenger

+Divides history into periods

+Shows conflict on a cosmic scale

ACTIVITY

Prepare matching cards with the information in the segments above, so participants can match the Greek to the English translation.

Learning Center Seven

NEVER-ENDING SONG

In John's vision, God Almighty, who created heaven and earth, is worshipped by angels and fantastic living creatures and people who lived before.

They all sing a never-ending song:

> *"Holy, Holy, Holy,*
> *Lord God Almighty..."*

Is this song familiar to you?

Canticles are songs from the Bible that are not Psalms. Revelation is punctuated with canticles, as these are glimpses of the ongoing worship that is occurring on a cosmic scale, despite any evil earth is enduring.

The canticles from *Revelation* can be printed out (perhaps on paper of a special shape or color) to post on the display. Be sure to include:

Rev. 4:8
Rev. 5:12
Rev. 5:13
Rev. 7:12
Rev. 11:17
Rev. 15:3-4

ACTIVITY

Mark hymnals with the texts that have been drawn directly from the liturgies or hymns in Revelation for the participants to peruse.
(For example, *"Crown Him with Many Crowns"*; *"Holy, Holy, Holy"*; *"What Wondrous Love Is This"*; *"At the Lamb's High Feast We Sing"*; *"Rejoice, O Pilgrim Throng"*; *"Open Now Thy Gates of Beauty"*; *"Jerusalem, My Happy Home"*; *"Ye Servants of God"*)

The concept of "rapture" is NEVER mentioned in the Book of Revelation. Instead, quite the opposite happens. God descends to earth to dwell with us in his perfect city—the New Jerusalem. You can read the description of this ideal place in the last two chapters of the Book of Revelation.

At last, God's creation will be perfect, with a wonderful, gleaming city, where God will live with us. The brightness of God will be so amazing, that the sun will not be needed for light any more!

When you worship, remember that you are part of the story, so join with all of creation to sing:

"Holy, Holy, Holy,
Lord God Almighty..."

And, add your prayer to John's:

"Come, Lord Jesus!"

ACTIVITY

Have a mural or a gigantic drawing of a tree. Have an assortment of twelve different types of stickers (actual pictures of fruits—or twelve different colors or circles—or white circles with twelve different colors of crayons for filling them in) that participants will place on the tree to represent the fruits on the Tree of Life. As a caption, print Rev. 22:1-2.

CREATION CELEBRATION

Instructions

This particular multigenerational event is designed for children of all ages. To hold a *Creation Celebration*, you will set up a table for each of the seven days of the story in the first chapter of Genesis. You might identify each table by a poster created from a collage of pictures that illustrates the particular aspects of creation for that day. Alternatively, the creation of such a collage could be one of the activities of each center. An appropriate craft selection would be offered at each center, ideas for which follow.

Refreshments Table

Possibilities are limited only by your imagination, but be sure to label your offerings!

Nectar of the Knowledge of Good & Evil (i.e. apple juice)
Name that Animal Cracker (i.e. animal crackers)
Gifts from God's Garden (i.e. fruit & veggie tray)
Multiplying Minnows (i.e. goldfish crackers)

Day One: Day & Night   **Genesis 1:1-6**

The poster collage would be pictures of celestial objects.

Craft One: *Crayon Scratch Drawings*, which are made by coloring an entire page randomly with assorted colors of crayon. Then, the whole page is colored again with black crayon. After that, take a pointed object and scratch away a drawing. The rainbow colors will show through. If you offer quarter-sized or half-sized paper, the project will not be overwhelming. Be sure to protect your table's surface with newspaper.

Craft Two: *Preprinted Scratch Paper Drawings* are similar to the activity described above, but they begin with purchased black sheets that are layered beneath with printed colors. The participants only need to scratch their designs to see the rainbow colors shine through. Such specialty paper is available at paper supply outlets or teacher supply stores.

Craft Three: *Blueprint Exposures*, for which you must obtain blueprint paper and make prints of assorted objects, following the directions on the package, by exposure to the sun.

Day Two: Land & Sea   **Genesis 1:7-8**

The poster collage would be pictures of lakes, oceans, and open landscapes (i.e. ones without any vegetation obvious).

Craft One: *Sponge-print Paintings* depend upon the purchase or creation of sponges in the shapes of fish and other sea creatures. Pour paint into trays. Have blue construction paper for the background. Participants sponge-paint underwater scenes.

Craft Two: *Homemade Ocean-in-a-Bottle* follows this recipe:
        Use a clean glass jar (one for each participant).
        Fill half of the jar with turpentine.
        Next add rubbing alcohol until the jar is almost full.
        Now add a few drops of blue food coloring.
        Glue the lid onto the jar, to prevent terrible accidents.
        When the glue is quite dry, tip the bottle from side-to-side, to
                watch the waves.

Day Three: Plants   **Genesis 1:9-13**

Poster collage of a variety of vegetation.

Craft One: *Seed Search* offers multiple types of fruits to be cut open to search for the seeds within.

Craft Two: *Seed Plantings*, in which everyone plants seeds into moistened soil in Ziploc bags. The see-through bags, when taped to a window, will enable the children to observe the sprouting.

Day Four: Stars   **Genesis 1:14-19**

Poster collage of constellations and other galactic phenomena.

Craft One: *Origami Stars* will depend upon instructions for folding origami stars from squares of paper. Alternatively, instructions could be offered for cutting a "Betsy Ross Star". Directions for either are available through internet searches.

Craft Two: *Glittery Night Paintings* simply offer black construction paper and glitter paint. An alternative to glitter paint would be star stickers.

Day Five: Creatures of the Sea & Air   **Genesis 1:20-23**

Poster collage of all types of flying and swimming animals.

Craft One: *Crayon Wash Drawings* are made by coloring the animals with crayon and then washing the entire page over with blue paint. This gives an underwater effect.

Craft Two: *Origami Animals* will depend upon finding instructions for these and providing squares of paper.

Day Six: Animals & Humans   **Genesis 1:24-31**

Poster Collage will be as varied as the pictures you can find of living creatures.

Craft One: *Mural of Life* begins with a roll of mural paper, such as the ends of newsprint from a newspaper publisher. Label sections with each letter of the alphabet. Participants then draw or name as many creatures as they can for each letter of the alphabet.

Craft Two: *Naming*, a fun search for particular names in a baby name book, in order to find out the meanings for these.

Day Seven: Rest & Sabbath   **Genesis 2:1-3**

Craft Idea: *Memory Bracelet* is made. Color-coded plastic beads are offered to be threaded upon cords, in order, and tied into bracelets. The colors of the beads stand for:
        White bead—Light from Day One
        Dark Blue bead—Water from Day Two
        Green bead—Plant life of Day Three
        Silver-bead—Starlight of Day Four
        Light Blue bead—Sky life of Day Five
        Red bead—Animals of Day Six
        Golden bead—Sabbath for Day Seven

UNIFYING CONCEPT

EX- MARKS THE SPOT

Is there a master plan? Are our human experiences archetypical? Humankind has always sought the answers to the big questions of life. Who are we? Why are we here? Why do we suffer? Why do we die? How do we cope? Are we alone in the universe?

For centuries, mortals have looked for answers in the Holy Bible. Do the generations of characters within those pages have relevance to our personal stories? How many stories would you say there are in the Bible? Hundreds? Thousands?

The biblical storyline leads us from creation, when evil first entered the human heart, to a resurrection to new life, when God will enter our hearts. But that journey has alternate paths, so where do we place ourselves? How do we find a story that matches our own?

For those who feel they have no control, who are enslaved to stronger forces, or who seek freedom, there is a great story of liberation in the Bible—the Exodus. Quite a lot of Old Testament ink is devoted to this storyline, but there are obvious parallels in the New Testament to a similar experience.

For those who feel isolated, alienated, or without a home, there is a great story of restoration, or homecoming, in the Bible—the Exile. A dominant storyline in the Old Testament, the theme of Exile may also be found in New Testament narratives.

For those who feel ashamed or guilt-ridden, there are great stories of reconciliation through sacrifice in the Bible, which might be termed Expiation, or Exculpation. This is an idea that originates in the Old Testament, but it finds full expression in the crucifixion of Jesus detailed in the New Testament.

One could even claim that every human problem may be identified within one of these three models. In other words, **Ex-** marks the spot, whether it be the **Ex**odus, the **Ex**ile, or **Ex**piation. These three narrative types represent three approaches that the Trinity of Father, Son, and Holy Spirit displays through Scripture.

The first, the Exodus storyline is based on a political model, offering the Law, through that great mediator, Moses. We are in bondage to sin, but God leads us from slavery to Sabbath.

The second, the storyline of the Exile, is founded through a prophetic model and offers the Truth, perhaps as represented by Elijah. We stray from the covenant to become strangers in a strange land, but an ever-faithful God leads us home again.

The third model, that of Expiation/Exculpation, presents a priestly approach, better understood as sacrifice, and Jesus Christ is the uppermost example. We cannot help ourselves, but God reaches out with atonement, once and for all.

A chart might look like this:

EX- MARKS the SPOT

EXODUS	**EXILE**	**EXPIATION**
Liberation Theme	Restoration Theme	Reconciliation Theme
Political Model	Prophetic Model	Priestly Model
Exemplar is Moses*	Exemplar is Elijah*	Exemplar is Christ Jesus*

*Here's a curiosity: Do you remember the figures in the Transfiguration story?

If you think about it, however, even these three meta-storylines can be condensed into one plot. God loved humankind; God lost humankind; God reaches out to win back humankind. That is the big picture. Thanks be to God!

UNIVERSAL CONSECRATION

UNIVERSAL CONSECRATIONS

"In Praise of Creation"

Leader   Let us give thanks for the earth—
                      Pebbles and prairies,
                      Forests and fields,
                      Tropics and tundra.
            Let all creation hear—

Response   Thanks be to God!

Leader   Let us give thanks for the water—
                      Currents and creeks,
                      Seaweed and seashells,
                      Waterfalls and waves.
            Let all creation hear—

Response   Thanks be to God!

Leader   Let us give thanks for the sky—
                      Raindrops and rainbows,
                      Snowflakes and sunsets,
                      Clouds and constellations.
            Let all creation hear—

Response   Thanks be to God!

Leader   Let us give thanks for the north—
                      Mists and meadowlarks,
                      Lakes and loons,
                      Cornfields and cardinals.
            Let all creation hear—

Response   Thanks be to God!

Leader   Let us give thanks for the east—
                      Estuaries and egrets,
                      Sand-dunes and sandpipers,
                      Hills and hemlocks.

	Let all creation hear—

Response   Thanks be to God!

Leader   Let us give thanks for the south—
        Magnolias and mockingbirds,
        Cotton and catfish,
        Deltas and dogwoods.
    Let all creation hear—

Response   Thanks be to God!

Leader   Let us give thanks for the west—
        Canyons and cactus,
        Mountains and magpies,
        Sagebrush and salmon.
    Let all creation hear—

Response   Thanks be to God!

Leader   Let us give thanks for all creatures—
        Kittens and kangaroos,
        Pandas and parrots,
        Elephants and eagles,
        Dragonflies and dolphins,
        And all humankind.
    Let all creation hear—

Response   Thanks be to God!

All   Amen and amen.

"In Your Holy Grasp"

Everlasting Creator,

Enlighten us by your Holy Grace,

Encourage us to seek your Holy Will,

Empower us with your Holy Spirit,

Employ us in your Holy Work,

Engage us as envoys of to your Holy Mission,

Embolden us as evangelists of your Holy Gospel,

Embrace us by your Holy Love,

Enliven us by your Holy Word,

Enfold us in your Holy Grasp forever,

Lead us into respectful communion with your Holy Creation,

Through the one who is able to keep us from falling and

Present us faultless before your glory with exceeding great joy,

Jesus Christ, Our Lord.

Amen.